The No-nonsense Guide to Born-digital Content

No-nonsense Guides

Facet's No-nonsense Guides are a set of straightforward practical working tools offering expert advice on a wide-range of topics. Simple to understand for those with little or no experience, the Guides provide pragmatic solutions to the problems facing library and information professionals today.

Other titles in this series:

The No-nonsense Guide to Archives and Recordkeeping
Margaret Crockett

The No-nonsense Guide to Legal Issues in Web 2.0 and Cloud Computing
Charles Oppenheim

The No-nonsense Guide to Training in Libraries
Barbara Allan

The No-nonsense Guide to Project Management
Barbara Allan

The No-nonsense Guide to Born-digital Content

Heather Ryan and Walker Sampson

Published by Facet Publishing
7 Ridgmount Street, London WC1E 7AE
www.facetpublishing.co.uk

Facet Publishing is wholly owned by CILIP:
the Library and Information Association.

British Library Cataloguing in Publication Data
A catalogue record for this book is available from the British Library.

ISBN 978-1-78330-195-9 (paperback)
ISBN 978-1-78330-196-6 (hardback)
ISBN 978-1-78330-256-7 (e-book)

First published 2018

Text printed on FSC accredited material.

Typeset from author's files in 11/14pt Revival 565 and Frutiger by Flagholme Publishing Services.
Printed and made in Great Britain by CPI Group (UK) Ltd, Croydon, CR0 4YY.

Contents

List of figures and tables ix

Foreword xi
Trevor Owens

Acknowledgements xv

List of abbreviations xix

Glossary xxi

Introduction 1
What is born-digital content? 1
Why is this important? 2
About the book 3
Additional resources 6
Representing the world of libraries and archives 6

1 Digital information basics 9
What is digital information? 9
Hexadecimal 12
Digital file types 12
Storage media 22
Command line basics 26
Code repositories 28
Conclusion 29
Further reading 30

2 Selection 31
Types of born-digital content 31

Format- versus content-driven collection decisions 36
Mission statements, collection policies and donor agreements 37
Gift agreements 44
Stanford University's approach to selection in web archiving 46
Conclusion 50
Further reading 50

3 Acquisition, accessioning and ingest 53
Principles of acquisition 53
Acquisition of born-digital material on a physical carrier 54
Checksums and checksum algorithms 69
Acquisition of network-born materials 71
Accession 83
Ingest 84
Conclusion 85
Further reading 85

4 Description 87
General fields and types of information 87
Descriptive standards and element sets 90
General element sets 99
Descriptive systems 101
Use cases 103
Conclusion 106
Further reading 107

5 Digital preservation storage and strategies 111
A note on acquisition 112
A note on file formats 112
Thinking about storage 114
Certification 121
Digital preservation policy 123
Conclusion 127
Further reading 127

6 Access 129
Deciding on your access strategy 129
Methods of access 145
Use case 148
Conclusion 149
Further reading 149

7 Designing and implementing workflows **153**
A note on tools 153
Design principles 154
Workflow and policy 159
Examples 160
Case study 161
Conclusion 162
Further reading 163

8 New and emerging areas in born-digital materials **165**
Storage 165
Software and apps 166
Cloud technologies 167
Smartphones 168
Digital art and new media 169
Emerging descriptive and access methods 169
Growing your skills 170
Conclusion 173
Further reading 174

Conclusion **177**

References **183**
Appendix A: Resources 187
Appendix B: Basic Unix command line prompts 193

Index **197**

List of figures and tables

Figures

1.1	A row of books and spaces representing binary information	10
1.2	Bitstream represented as a 15 pixel/inch bitmapped image	15
1.3	Pixels encoded in the Red (R), Green (G), and Blue (B) colour space	16
1.4	A simple vector line with beginning and endpoints with Bézier curve adjusters	17
1.5	Our friend, the sloth, as a vector graphic	18
1.6	A sound wave as it is detected by a microphone, sampled and translated into digital information	19
1.7	Three tables in a relational database showing the relationships between the Favourite Animal (FavAnimalNum) and Creator (CreatorNum) fields between the tables	21
3.1	If the 3.5″ write tab is covered, the disk is *write-enabled*	57
3.2	If the 5.25″ notch is covered, the disk is *write-protected*	58
3.3	If the 8″ notch is covered – or not present – the disk is *write-enabled*	58
3.4	Snippet of hex editor display of a JPEG image file	65
3.5	Snippet of hex editor display of a disk image file	65
3.6	Eight-inch floppy disk with significant labelling and creator marks	67
4.1	An OCLC MARC record describing floppy disks	104
4.2	Screenshot of a digital object described in ArchivesSpace using DACS with additional digital object specific fields	104
4.3	PREMIS metadata for a TARGA image of a hand	105
5.1	Overview diagram of the OAIS model	122
7.1	A basic input–output pipeline for a media capture and ingest	156
7.2	Slide from 'Arrangement and Description for Born Digital Materials'	157
7.3	Workflow at Johns Hopkins University with two automation steps	158

Tables

1.1 Binary/ASCII text/Hexadecimal conversion chart 11
4.1 Comparison of born-digital information needs across descriptive standards and element sets 102

Foreword

Catching up to the present: join the born-digital community of practice

When historians tell stories of life in the latter half of the 20th and beginnings of the 21st century they will do so from an evidentiary basis of born-digital primary sources: e-mails, websites, Word documents, PDFs, video and audio files. It is from born-digital objects like these that people of the future will come to understand our world. I continue to use the somewhat awkward phrase 'born digital' because for most library, archives and museum professionals digitisation remains their default conception of what digital collection content is. That needs to change. We need to catch up to the digital present and I think *The No-nonsense Guide to Born-digital Content* can help us.

Librarians, archivists and museum professionals need to collectively move away from thinking about digital, and in particular born-digital, as being niche topics for specialists. If our institutions are to meet the mounting challenges of serving the cultural memory functions of an increasingly digital-first society the institutions themselves need to transition to become digital-first themselves. We can't just keep hiring a handful of people with the word 'digital' in their job titles. You don't go to a digital doctor to get someone who uses computing as part of their medical practice, and we can't expect that the digital archivists are the ones who will be the people who do digital things in archives. The things this book covers are things that all cultural heritage professionals need to get up to speed on.

I am thrilled to have the chance to open Heather and Walker's book. I have known both of them directly and indirectly through our shared travels through the world of digital preservation. In what follows I offer a few of my thoughts and observations for you to take with you as you work through this book on a journey into the growing digital preservation community of practice.

To kick off your exploration of this book I will lay out three observations that I believe are essential to this journey: we will never catch up, our biggest risk is inaction and we all need to get beyond the screen in our understanding of digital information. Together, I believe these points demonstrate the need to use this book as a stepping stone, a jumping-off point for joining the community of practice engaged in the craft of digital preservation.

'Forever catching up to the present': I've borrowed part of the title of my foreword from a talk that Michael Edson, then the Director of Web Strategy for the Smithsonian Institution, gave several years ago. In that talk Edson implored digital preservation practitioners to help their institutions catch up to the present. I've heard many talk about 'the digital revolution' like it was a singular thing that happened. It wasn't. Instead we have entered something that for the time being at least looks more like a permanent state of digital revolution. Punch cards, mainframes, PCs, the internet, the web, social media, mobile computing, computer vision and now things like voice-based interfaces and the internet of things: all varying and distinct elements in the continually changing digital landscape. It doesn't seem like we will land in a new normal; or if there is a new normal, it's to expect a constantly changing digital knowledge ecosystem. In this context, there is much for librarians to teach and much for us to learn. We need to move more and more into a state of continual professional learning. We need to be improving our digital skills by engaging in professional development and by taking on ways to become experts in new areas. This book can help you do that. In what follows I will briefly suggest two ways.

Inaction as one of our biggest risks: There is no time to wait. Digital media is more unstable and more complex than what most media librarians, archivists and curators have worked with. We don't have time for a new generation of librarians and archivists to move into the field. We don't have time for everyone to do years of professional development. Instead, we need to make space and time for working cultural heritage professionals to start engaging in the practices of digital curation. This book can be a huge help in this regard.

Get beyond the screen: Digital information isn't just what it looks like on the screen at a given moment. To be an information professional in an increasingly digital world requires all of us to get beyond the screens in two key ways. First, we all need to develop a base-level conceptual understanding of the nature of digital information. This book is helpful in that regard by providing some foundational context for understanding bitstreams and data structures. Second, we need to up our game for working with command line tools and scripts. As the pace of change around digital information develops and changes we can't depend on the development of tools with slick graphic user interfaces. We need to accept that all the systems and platforms we use are layers of and interfaces to our digital assets. That is, your content isn't 'in' whatever repository system you use; that system needs to be best understood as the current interface layer that effectively floats on top of the digital assets to which you are ensuring long-term access. The hands-on focus of this book and the inclusion of methods and techniques for working with data at the command line are invaluable as a jumping-off point for learning this kind of skill and technique.

Embracing the craft

When I started working in digital preservation more than a decade ago I was largely confused and befuddled by a field that presented points of entry to the work as complex technical specifications and system requirements documents. It felt like there were a lot of people talking about how the work should be done and not a lot of people doing the work that needed to be done. I've been very excited to see the field turn that corner in the last decade.

We are moving further and further away from the idea that digital preservation is a technical problem that the right system can solve and toward the realisation that ensuring long-term access to digital information is a craft that we practise and refine by doing the work. I think this book can help us all become better reflective digital preservation practitioners. However, it can only do that if you actually start to practise the craft. So do that. If you aren't already, go ahead and start to participate, and join the community that is forming around these practices.

You can use this book to help you to start learning by doing. You will get the most value out of the book if you are trying to work through the process of getting, describing, managing and providing access to digital content. As you go along, you are going to need to write down what you are doing and why you are doing it the way you are. One of my mentors,

Martha Anderson, would always describe digital preservation as a relay race. You're just one of the first runners in a great chain of runners carrying content forward into the future. When those folks in the future inherit your content they are going to need to understand why you did what you did with it, and the only way they are going to be able to do that is by reading the documentation you produced regarding the how and the why of all the choices you made. So be sure to write that down. I would also implore you to share what you write as you go.

Around every corner there is another new kind of content. There is another challenging issue regarding privacy, ethics and personal information. There is another set of questions about how to describe and make content discoverable. There is another new kind of digital format, another new interface and another new form of digital storage. You can't do this alone. The good news is that everyone working on these issues in libraries, archives, museums, non-profits, government and companies can share what we figure out as we work through this process and build a global knowledge base of information about this work together. Take this book as a jumping-off point.

Join digital preservation-focused organizations like the National Digital Stewardship Alliance, the Research Data Alliance, the International Internet Preservation Consortium, the Electronic Records Section of the Society of American Archivists and the Digital Preservation Coalition. Go to their conferences, start following people involved in these groups on Twitter, follow their journals, their blogs and their e-mail lists.

It's dangerous to go alone! Take this book as the starting point of a journey into our community of practice and realise that you are not alone. Even if it really is just you working on digital preservation as a lone arranger at a small organization the rest of us are out here working away at the same problems.

Trevor Owens
Head, Digital Content Management
Library of Congress

Acknowledgements

I am so pleased to be able to bring this book to the profession. During the years that I was teaching library, archives and information science, I always felt the need for a book like this. It is with tremendous support and a few surprising turns of events that I find myself now reminiscing in how I wound up here and who helped me along the way.

This all started when I was preparing to teach my *Introduction to Archives and Records Management* class. I had pre-ordered Laura Millar's *Archives: Principles and practices* book for the class. As the first day of class drew nearer, I began regularly checking if the order had arrived. It hadn't yet, and as it turns out, there was such a high demand for the book that it was sold out in every venue. I became bold in my desperation, and I sent a tweet to Laura Millar's Twitter account to ask her if she knew whether more were on the way. She quickly responded and tagged her publisher, who happened to be Facet Publishing. On the double, Facet dispatched copies of the book, and all was well.

Not too long after this event, I received an e-mail from Damian Mitchell, Commissioning Editor at Facet Publishing. It turns out that my tweet to Ms Millar alerted him to my existence. Like any responsible commissioning editor, he followed the lead, read my CV, and then sent me an e-mail inviting me to submit a book proposal. I was a little surprised, but my surprise was almost immediately replaced by a sense of need and great opportunity. I had recently taught my Advanced Archives course where I covered managing born-digital collections. Throughout the course, I felt the absence of a good, overarching text on the subject. I knew then that I had to propose this book.

So, my first acknowledgement is to Laura Millar. First, for writing such an excellent book on the principles and practices of archives – really, truly one of the BEST books on the topic! – and second, for being the unsuspecting gateway to this opportunity. I would also like to acknowledge and thank Damian Mitchell for turning my tiny plea in the Twitterverse into a door leading to the wonderful world of book writing. Damian is a gem: always kind, supportive and engaged. I could not have asked for a better editor.

The next person I would like to acknowledge is my intrepid co-author, Walker Sampson. But first, let me tell you a little story. Damian and his colleagues at Facet accepted my proposal and I was all set to write the book over the summer, between teaching quarters. By the time summer arrived, I had made the decision to branch out and begin a new archival and digital preservation consulting career. This was a change, but I still felt confident that I could write the book over the summer along with the few consulting jobs I had going. One of the jobs, however, was for the University of Colorado (CU) Boulder Libraries' Special Collections and Archives Department.

The summer came and went as I found myself stepping in full time as the Acting Head of Archives at CU Boulder. Not too long after that, my husband and I sold our house and moved to be closer to Boulder. And not long after that, I applied for and was offered the role of CU Boulder Libraries' Director of Special Collections, Archives and Preservation Department. As I shifted through so much change, and as I took on more responsibilities, I knew that I could not write this book on my own. About six months into the process, I reached out to Walker, CU Boulder's Digital Archivist and my respected colleague, to help me out. He jumped on board without batting an eyelid, and I couldn't be more grateful. I honestly could not have done this without him.

I also could not have done this without my two dear mentors, Drs Cal Lee and Helen Tibbo. They both taught me and provided me with the opportunity to learn just about everything I know about managing born-digital collections. I credit them with everything I got right, and claim anything I've missed or misconstrued here as solely my own doing. I would also like to thank my CU Boulder Libraries Deans, everyone in the Special Collections, Archives and Preservation Department, all of the other wonderful people I work with at the Libraries and across the CU Boulder campus, all of my incredible colleagues across the globe, and my bright and passionate students, who are all becoming impressive colleagues in their own right.

I would also like to thank Trevor Owens, who has been a great friend and guiding light throughout many stages of my career. I am thrilled and honoured to have him kick off the book with his foreword. And thanks to Jim Kalwara for help with the MARC record example and to Jane Thaler for her last-minute help with ArchivesSpace and quotes. Thank you also to Steina and Woody Vasulka for providing us with such wonderful use case material and for giving us permission to feature some of your material in the book.

Last, but far from least, I would like to thank my husband, Joe. He's been a true partner to me every step of the way up to and through writing this book. A testament to his dedication is the fact that he made sure that I was fed, the house was clean and the dog was walked these many months. Thank you, Joe.

Heather Ryan

I would like to thank my co-author for inviting me on board this book – it's been a true pleasure. I nearly jumped (literally) at the opportunity to write whole chapters on the work that occupies my day-to-day. I want to also thank my professors at the University of Texas at Austin's School of Information, who have been critical to my knowledge and growth. Special thanks to Dr Patricia Galloway and Dr Megan Winget for indulging me in all the various projects and papers I endeavoured. Thanks as well to all the folks at the Maryland Institute of Technology in the Humanities – a brief stint there in the sweltering Maryland summer taught me untold amounts, and in great company. Many thanks as well to the wonderful colleagues I've worked with over the years, here at the University of Colorado and at the Mississippi Department of Archives and History – you all are fundamental to any good work issuing from this corner of the field. And I want to thank Russ Corley, former director of the Goodwill Computer Museum, for allowing me to learn on the job – a lot.

Finally, many thanks to my family and friends for their love and support.

Walker Sampson

List of abbreviations

AACR	Anglo-American Cataloging Rules
APFS	Apple File System
API	application programming interface
ASCII	American Standard Code for Information Interchange
CMS	content management system
CNI	Coalition for Network Information
CRL	Center for Research Libraries
CSV	Comma Separated Value
DACS	Describing Archives: a Content Standard
DRM	digital rights management
DROID	Digital Record Object Identification
EWF	Expert Witness Compression Format
FAT	File Allocation Table
FRBR	Functional Requirements for Bibliographic Records
FTP	File Transfer Protocol
GUI	Graphical User Interface
HFS	Hierarchical File system
HTML	HyperText Markup Language
HTTP	Hypertext Transfer Protocol
IIPC	International Internet Preservation Consortium
ISAD(G)	General International Standard Archival Description
ISBD	International Standard Bibliographic Description
ISBD (ER)	International Standard Bibliographic Description for Electronic Resources
ISO	International Standards Organization
IT	information technology
LTFS	Linear Tape File System
MAD	Manual of Archival Description

MARC	Machine Readable Cataloging
MIME	Multipurpose Internet Mail Extensions
NDSA	National Digital Stewardship Alliance
NLP	natural language processing
NTFS	New Technology File System
OAIS	Open Archival Information System Reference Model
OCLC	Online Computer Library Center
OPF	Open Preservation Foundation
PC	personal computer
PDF	Portable Document Format
PII	personally identifying information
RAD	Rules for Archival Description
RDA	Resource Description and Access
RGB	red, green and blue
TRAC	*Trustworthy Repositories Audit & Certification*
UDF	Universal Disk Format
XML	eXtensible Markup Language

Glossary

Accessibility: a measure of how products or systems are designed for people who experience disability.

Accessioning: integrating the content into your archives: e.g. assigning an identifier to the accession, associating the accession with a collection and adding this administrative information into your inventory or collection management system.

Acquisition: physical retrieval or capture of digital content. This could describe acquiring files from a floppy drive, selecting files off of a donor's hard drive or receiving files as an e-mail attachment from a donor.

Advanced Forensics Format (AFF): an open format designed to contain disk images and associated metadata.

American Standard Code for Information Interchange (ASCII): a character encoding standard commonly used in English-based text documents.

Anglo-American Cataloging Rules (AACR): rules for cataloguing bibliographic and other materials developed and used in primarily English-speaking libraries.

Archival Information Package: an information package comprised of a digital object and its associated metadata; part of the Open Archival Information System (OAIS) Reference Model.

Bézier curve: a parametric curve used to create digital graphics, most commonly in vector graphics illustrations.

BIBFRAME: a data model for bibliographic description utilising linked data, designed to replace the MARC 21 descriptive standard.

Bit: a basic unit of binary information used in digital communication.

BitCurator Access: a product designed to provide web-based access to content encoded in disk images. It also provides redaction capabilities and emulation services.

BitCurator Environment: a suite of open source digital forensics and analysis tools oriented to processing born-digital materials in cultural heritage contexts.

Bitmap image: a digital image composed of a matrix of pixels.

Born-digital: information created and recorded at its inception in electronic form.

Byte: eight bits of data.

Checksum: the output of an algorithm designed to calculate a cryptographic hash that is used to uniquely identify a set of data and to determine if errors have been introduced to that data during storage or transmission; may also be used to detect intentional changes to digital files and to discover duplicate files. Common checksum algorithms are MD5, SHA1 and SHA2 (a family of functions containing SHA-224, SHA-256, SHA-384 and SHA-512).

Collection policy: the definition of selection criteria for libraries and archives as they relate to the institutional priorities and mission.

Command line: a method of interacting with computer functions and programs by entering typed commands into a text console.

CONTENTdm: a digital content management system with a robust discovery interface, provided by the Online Computer Library Center, Incorporated.

Data Seal of Approval: a series of guidelines developed by Data Archiving and Networked Services of the Netherlands to help ensure that archived data is discoverable and useful over time, succeeded by CoreTrustSeal.

Describing Archives: a Content Standard (DACS): a set of rules and guidelines for describing primarily archival material, managed by the Society of American Archivists.

Descriptive standard: a set of guidelines or rules to direct the representation of information related to archival or library material in a catalogue or archival finding aid.

Digital: refers to information that is expressed in digits, or numbers; more specifically the numbers 1 and 0.

Digital Commons: a hosted institutional repository platform.

Digital forensics: a branch of criminal forensic science in which evidence of criminal activity is sought on digital devices, many of the tools and procedures of which have been adapted for use in digital archives processes.

Digital object: a set of binary information that has a defined structure and can be rendered in a meaningful way by using associated software and hardware.

Digital Record Object Identification (DROID): a file format identification tool developed by the UK National Archives that references the PRONOM file signature database.

Digital watermarking: a mark or signal inserted into a digital image, audio file or video file that indicates copyright ownership of the content.

Disk image: a computer file containing a full-sector copy of a digital storage device such as a floppy disk or hard disk drive.

Dissemination Information Package: an information package received by an entity that requested it; part of the Open Archival Information System Reference Model.

Donor agreement: an agreement between the person or party donating collection materials and the institution receiving the gift in which the ownership of the physical and sometimes intellectual property is legally transferred to the receiving party.

Drupal: an open source content management system that can be used for a number of online content hosting scenarios.

DSpace: an open source repository package with a focus on long-term storage, access and preservation of digital content.

Dublin Core: a simplified metadata element set comprised of 15 core elements: Title, Creator, Subject, Description, Publisher, Contributor, Date, Type, Format, Identifier, Source, Language, Relation, Coverage and Rights.

Element set: a standard set of metadata fields used for describing various materials, including archival and library content.

Emulator: software designed to reproduce the functions and operations of another machine, operating system or software.

ePADD: a system created to process, describe, host and provide access to e-mail collections.

EPrints: open source software for building open access repositories.

Expert Witness Compression Format (EWF): a type of disk image that contains a copy of a digital storage device along with added metadata and optional lossless compression.

File system: a method for controlling how digital data is stored and retrieved on various digital storage media. Examples include: FAT (FAT12, FAT16, FAT32), exFAT, LTFS, NTFS, HFS and HFS+, HPFS,

APFS, UFS, ext2, ext3, ext4, XFS, btrfs, ISO 9660, Files-11, Veritas File System, VMFS, ZFS, ReiserFS and UDF.

Finding aid: a document that records the arrangement, structure and contextual information of archival collections and serves as a discovery aid for these collections.

Floppy disk: a storage medium made of a thin, flexible, circular piece of plastic coated with a thin layer of magnetic material, encased in a harder plastic container; used primarily from the 1980s to the 1990s.

Format Identification for Digital Objects (fido): a command line tool to identify digital file formats.

Functional requirements: a list of a system's necessary behaviours which are used in a designing process to define needs the system must address.

Functional Requirements for Bibliographic Records (FRBR): a conceptual-relationship model developed by the International Federation of Library Associations that describes an entity's levels as a work, expression, manifestation and item.

General International Standard Archival Description (ISAD(G)): a standard that defines the elements used to describe archival material; designed for international application and used as a standard with which other standards attempt to comply.

Graphical user interface (GUI): Often pronounced 'gooey', a system of images and text that facilitates interaction with a computer or software.

Hexadecimal: a digital encoding system that uses 16 characters represented by the numbers 0–9 and the letters A, B, C, D, E and F; often used as a secondary notation after binary encoding where a pair of hexadecimal values equals a single byte.

Ingest: the process of placing your content into a repository system for digital content.

International Standard Bibliographic Description (ISBD): a set of rules for describing bibliographic content.

Islandora: an open source software framework that combines Fedora, Drupal and Solr technologies to manage and provide access to digital content.

JSTOR/Harvard Object Validation Environment (JHOVE): a format-specific file validation tool.

KryoFlux: a hardware and software package developed to help create disk images of disks of almost any size and format.

Machine Readable Cataloging (MARC): a set of standards for bibliographic description designed to be processed by computers.

Magnetic media: a type of digital storage media that operates by using a magnet to change the polarity of atoms contained in a thin layer of magnetic material, typically iron-oxide, to either north or south polarity, which is read as either a zero or a one in binary information systems.

Manual of Archival Description (MAD): guidelines for creating finding aid documents for archival collections, used primarily in the UK.

Migration: a method of preserving access to digital files by transferring them from an old, unsupported file format to a contemporary, supported file format.

Mission statement: a summary of an institution's primary goals and values.

More Product, Less Process (MPLP): an archival processing philosophy that supports the idea of processing and describing more collections at a higher level, versus processing fewer collections at a deeper, more complete level.

Network-born: digital content that is routinely accessed online and is primarily designed to operate through networks, such as websites, e-mail and social media content (Twitter posts, Facebook walls and Instagram photos).

Omeka: an open source web publishing or digital exhibit platform designed for libraries, archives, museums and scholars.

Open Archival Information System (OAIS) Reference Model: a conceptual framework for a digital collection ingest, storage, preservation and access system.

Optical media: a type of digital storage media that operates by using a laser to create tiny bubbles and pits in a thin layer of plastic on a disc such that light will either be reflected back to a reader or not; this is read as either a zero or a one in binary information systems.

Original order: the arrangement of archival records or manuscript material in which it was either first created or arranged later by the creator or owner; the arrangement of archival records or manuscript material in which it arrives as an acquisition at a collecting institution.

Personally identifiable information (PII): data about an individual that can be used to ascertain the identity, locate, contact or assume the identity of that person.

PREMIS: full title the 'PREMIS Data Dictionary for Preservation Metadata', an international descriptive standard for preservation metadata managed by the Library of Congress.

PRONOM: a technical registry provided by the UK National Archives.

Provenance: a record of creation and ownership of archival content.

Regular expression: a sequence of characters that delineate search patterns commonly used to locate phone numbers, e-mail addresses, identification numbers and other personally identifiable information.

Resource Description and Access (RDA): a descriptive standard for cataloguing bibliographic materials, designed to replace the AACR2 descriptive standard.

Respect des fonds: a principle that advises the grouping of collections by the body (roughly, the 'fonds') under which they were created and purposed. The two natural objectives flowing from *respect des fonds* are the retention of both provenance and original order.

RODA: an open source digital preservation repository.

Rules for Archival Description (RAD): a content standard for archival description developed and used primarily in Canada.

Samvera: an open source repository application designed for libraries and archives.

Siegfried: a signature-based file format identification tool.

Significant properties: those properties of a digital object that are important to the interpretation of its content.

Solid-state storage: a type of digital storage media that operates without the use of moving mechanical parts by using electronic circuits to produce negative and positive charges, which are read as either a zero or a one in binary information systems.

Submission Information Package (SIP): an information package as it is ingested into an archival system; part of the Open Archival Information System Reference Model.

Trusted Digital Repository (TDR) Checklist: an International Standards Organization (ISO) standard (16363) designed to guide the development of a digital repository that is reliable and trusted by the community that it serves.

Unicode Transformation Format-8 (UTF-8): a character encoding format that uses 8-bit blocks to transform binary information into human-readable symbols.

Unified Modeling Language (UML): a shared schema of shapes and visual cues to indicate a great deal of the logic you may find or want to display in a workflow: decision points, relationships and dependencies, among numerous others.

User requirement: a documented potential system utiliser need that is used to direct the design of a system.

User-centred design: a set of procedures for developing systems that place the potential users' requirements at the forefront of system design.

Vector image: a form of digital graphic that utilises shapes and geometric specifications to define the impression that is rendered on screen.

Wayback Machine: an initiative of the Internet Archive, a US-based non-profit that has accrued a large collection of archived websites, among other materials.

WordPress: an open source content management system.

Write blocker: a device that prevents all write commands issuing to any connected partition or device; also termed a forensic bridge.

Introduction

For tens of millennia humankind has made purposeful, material marks on whatever surface was available. Human beings have recorded evidence of their existence with ground rock smeared on cave walls, carvings in stone, plant fluids brushed onto papyrus, gold and coloured inks painted on animal skin, dark inks rolled onto movable type and pressed into paper, and magnetised iron oxide on a plastic substrate disk. These artefacts, whether they can be read ten minutes or ten millennia from now are all evidence of humans attempting the often Herculean feat of making sense of the world around them. No matter the medium, we are fixing our ideas and creations into a form that will allow them to move into the future. Over time, the content has been relatively similar, but the quantity and methods of recording this content have changed drastically.

In our current age, nearly all data and creative outputs are generated, stored and accessed through the use of computers. Records of our transactions, of our communication and experiences with one another, of our thoughts, ideas and creative outputs are almost all created, stored and transmitted via digital encoding. How much of your own communication and work is transacted or recorded digitally? More importantly for the library and archival professions, how do we go about collecting, preserving and providing access to it? This question may seem difficult or daunting to answer, but we can make it simple for you by starting with the basics and building from there.

What is born-digital content?

Photographs, books and maps created and printed on paper-based mediums can be 'digitised'. For the past few decades digitised content has been in high demand and a game-changer for libraries and archives' ability to share their resources across the globe. Digitising valuable and fragile materials reduces handling and therefore helps preserve the originals for longer periods of time.

Recently, however, more attention has been directed toward the content that is being created, distributed and used solely in digital form. This content is called 'born digital' because it was created or 'born' digitally, and in most cases is not transferred or accessed otherwise. Because there is no original paper-based or analogue version of born-digital content, it poses some unique challenges in preserving access to it over the long term.

Think about everything you create on a computer or digital device in a day. Every single type of digital file you create is within the purview of what can be collected and managed in libraries and archives. This can be as obvious as Microsoft Word documents and the JPEG images you take with your mobile phone, but what about the text messages on your phone or your e-mails? What about all of the content on your social media sites like Facebook and Instagram? Websites, complex databases, 3D animations, layered architectural drawings, whole films and a wide swathe of art also find their way into digital libraries and archives. There are literally thousands of types of digital content that are created first in digital form, and so there are thousands of types of born-digital content you may find yourself managing. If you are beginning to feel intimidated, please don't be! This book is filled with the basic, no-nonsense information you need to feel comfortable taking on the tremendously important work of collecting, preserving and providing access to born-digital content.

Why is this important?

This may seem obvious, but it is worth noting the importance of this kind of work. We just asked you to think of all of the different types of digital content you create on a daily basis. Now think about all of the content you create overall, and what percentage of that is digital. How many handwritten letters do you write and how many e-mails do you send? Even better, out of all the words you write, how many are digital? Now think about this on a global scale. How much of our cultural and scientific heritage is being recorded in digital form right now?

At this very moment the library and archives professions are in the middle of a monumental transition from the traditional methods of recording, storing and providing access to information, to an almost entirely new method predicated on ones and zeros. We've had hundreds of years to understand and perfect paper-based information storage and transmission methods. While digital information has been around for approaching 100 years, we are still relatively new at figuring out how to manage it effectively.

Because of this, and because we as a profession will be tasked with managing an increasing percentage of digital content, it is imperative that more of us pick up the knowledge and skills required to do it. We've heard anecdotally of the trepidation among not only established professionals, but also young librarians and archivists just beginning their career. Many think that because they don't possess a master's degree in computer science, they could not possibly take on this kind of work. We're here to tell you that this simply isn't true. We've seen aspiring archivists who thrill at the touch and smell of old documents, who claim to have no technical skills whatsoever, successfully create disk images from 3.5" floppy disks, install and run VirtualBox and BitCurator, and then proceed to run and analyse digital forensics reports.

To understand the informational content of most physical materials in libraries and archives, you don't need to know how ink and paper were made in order to interpret the messages printed on paper (you *do* need that knowledge to preserve and conserve them though!). In other words, you only need to know how to interpret the lines and symbols as letters and numbers and translate them in your mind into something meaningful that you could communicate verbally or in writing. To manage born-digital content, however, you could be initially successful without understanding the basics of how digital information is created, but your success will be limited. To be a knowledgeable born-digital content manager, you do need an understanding of how digital content is created and rendered into meaningful information. This isn't the simplest thing to do in the world, but it's not rocket science either. Most importantly, managing born-digital content will eventually become the core function of information management in libraries and archives. It is deeply important that these professions begin to pick up the knowledge and skills to do it well.

About the book

This book is written for librarians and archivists who have found themselves managing or are planning to manage born-digital content. We focus on those who have been working in the profession for a while and who may feel somewhat unsure of their ability to take on a task that by all appearances demands a high level of technological expertise. We also address this book to people who are new to these professions and who would like to acquire some basic knowledge about the topic. We hope that the book will make a good accompanying text for course and workshop instructors. Lastly, we think that it will be a useful book for those generally interested in the topic and who want to pick up some basic knowledge that they can apply to their work and life.

Our goal is to provide an introduction to the topic of managing born-digital content in library and archives settings, though we imagine that this information can be useful for museum, data repository and institutional records management environments. When we say 'basic' we really do mean basic in that we are presenting foundational knowledge from which you can continue to develop and learn. This book is meant to get you started on a deeper journey into the subject, or at the very least to satisfy a basic need or curiosity on the subject. Within this goal, we attempt to break down complex or technical subjects into simple, easy-to-digest parts.

Though we hail from academia, we have worked hard to avoid overly academic terminology and tone. We take the 'no nonsense' part of the book title very seriously, though we try to keep to a light-hearted tone, and *may* have snuck in a point or two of nonsense (but hopefully our editors don't notice!). We know that this topic can feel intimidating at first, and our true goal is to dispel the myth that only hard-core computer programmer types are suited to manage born-digital content. We believe that with the right introduction, anyone is capable of being a great born-digital content manager.

The book has eight core chapters book-ended by a foreword by Trevor Owens, Head of Digital Content Management at the Library of Congress, a glossary, this introduction, a conclusion, appendices and an index. The core chapters are as below and cover the following content.

Chapter 1 – Digital information basics. This chapter introduces basic concepts related to digital information, various file formats (websites, e-mail, mobile phone records, documents, spreadsheets, databases, images, video audio, etc.) and digital storage media (electromagnetic, optical and solid state storage media). It also covers some command line basics and an introduction to code repositories. The goal of this chapter is to introduce you to some of the basic concepts that drive how digital information works, so that you can have a strong understanding of the forces that shape the world of born-digital content management.

Chapter 2 – Selection. This chapter describes various sources of born-digital content for libraries and archives. It explores various strategies for making collecting decisions, which include mission statements, collecting policies and donor agreements. It discusses and provides examples of policies that address appraisal and collecting decisions which are particular to born-digital content, and provides an example donor agreement and addendum designed to address born-digital content specific needs.

Chapter 3 – Acquisition, accessioning and ingest. This chapter describes the steps that should be taken to retrieve and prepare the born-digital content to be officially brought into the library or archives. These steps include using write blockers to prevent processing systems from automatically writing to donated media, creating a disk image or complete copy of the storage media, methods to acquire digital content over a network and generating checksums to establish authenticity.

Chapter 4 – Description. This chapter discusses how information about born-digital collections can be collected to describe the content within different library and archives descriptive systems. It reviews available descriptive standards and element sets and compares them across a set of ideal types of metadata that one should collect for born-digital content specific description needs. It also provides a brief overview of current bibliographic, archival and digital repository descriptive systems.

Chapter 5 – Digital preservation storage and strategies. This chapter describes how a library or archives can apply preservation practices to its born-digital collections. We also discuss key considerations in storage, budgeting and policies. Additionally, this chapter explores the criteria covered by the Trusted Digital Repository and the Data Seal of Approval or CoreTrustSeal certifications, and how these certification programmes can fit into your preservation programme.

Chapter 6 – Access. This chapter discusses approaches to providing access to born-digital content and describes considerations for limitations to access such as privacy and copyrights in library and archives domains.

Chapter 7 – Designing and implementing workflows. This chapter describes strategies for designing full or partial workflows for born-digital collection processing, provides examples of these approaches in several different contexts and collections and introduces a few key considerations when thinking about workflows.

Chapter 8 – New and emerging areas in born-digital materials. This chapter discusses strategies and philosophies to move forward nimbly as technologies and the field change over the years. It examines new frontiers of digital storage, ways of creating digital content and methods of serving it up to your users. It also explores additional skills and knowledge that you may consider picking up to build up your born-digital content management toolkit.

Additional resources

As with any introductory book, the content within this No-nonsense Guide is just the tip of the iceberg of the information available on the topic. We include a 'Further reading' section at the end of every chapter to connect you with chapter-specific information that you can seek out and use to expand your knowledge on the subject presented. We also include a list of broader resources (Appendix A) that you can use to learn more and to connect with communities of practice that can be additional valuable sources of information. Considering the fact that this area of practice and research is continually evolving, the growing network of those doing work with born-digital content may be one of the richest and most valuable resources available to you. Please note, however, that we don't include every book, journal article or resource available on the topic, but aim to give you just enough to take the next step of growing your knowledge.

Representing the world of libraries and archives

We acknowledge that this book is intended for use throughout the world, and as such we have made every effort to make it as generalised as possible, so that, wherever you are, you can apply the knowledge we present to your situation. We try to provide examples culled from all over the globe and offer what we hope to be generic use cases that can be applicable within as many different institutional environments as possible.

All this being said, both of us are from the USA and work in the Special Collections, Archives and Preservation Department at the University of Colorado Boulder Libraries. While we work very hard to break out of our own bubbles, we acknowledge the fact that the knowledge we have to present has been undeniably shaped by our backgrounds. We apologise in advance for any American and archives-centric slant there may be to the book. We believe that the core content should shine through, nevertheless.

CHAPTER 1

Digital information basics

> Computers are the most complex objects we human beings have ever created, but in a fundamental sense they are remarkably simple.
>
> (Danny Hillis, *The Pattern on the Stone*, 1998, vii)

Learning how to preserve, conserve and describe paper-based materials usually entails learning about what the paper is made of and how it was made. It also involves knowing how the ink was made and how it was applied to the paper. Interpreting messages fixed on paper also requires an understanding of the language in which the messages were written, which also requires knowledge of the shapes and symbols used in the language represented. Understanding the basics of preserving and interpreting born-digital information is no different. It helps to understand how digital information is encoded and fixed onto physical media to make informed decisions about how best to preserve and provide access to it.

This chapter explains basic encoding methods used to convert various types of information into digital form, describes how digital information is fixed onto physical mediums and discusses basics of the command line and navigating code repositories. This may feel like an intimidating chapter to start with, but once you understand the concepts presented here, the rest of the principles and processes presented throughout the book will be simple to master.

What is digital information?

At a basic level, the word digital refers to information that is expressed in digits, or numbers; more specifically the numbers 1 and 0. The numbers 1 and 0 represent any kind of binary information presentation. This can be the presence (1) or absence (0) of something, different orientations of something like up (1) or down (0), statements of truth like TRUE (1) or FALSE (0), polar orientation like North (1) or South (0), dashes (1) or dots (0) like in Morse code; basically anything that can be represented by a maximum of two different states. Since digital information is encoded into only one of two digits, it is also referred to as 'binary' encoding, where 'bi' means 'two'. Each individual digit (a 1 or a 0) is called a 'bit'. A string of eight bits is called a 'byte'. To demonstrate this concept in my classes, I often line up a row of books along the whiteboard with seemingly random spaces in between and then draw slots for empty spaces, as you can see in Figure 1.1.

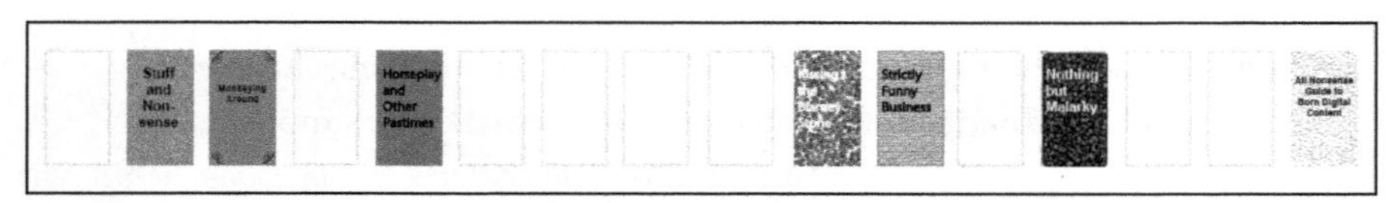

Figure 1.1 *A row of books and spaces representing binary information*

If you represent each book as a 1 and each empty space as a 0, you will have the following string of 'bits':

```
0110100001101001
```

Creations such as words, images, numerical data, music and videos can be captured or transferred into binary form through the use of any variety of binary encoding systems, or what we commonly call file formats. A simple and fairly well-known encoding system is the American Standard Code for Information Interchange, or ASCII. Table 1.1 opposite shows the ASCII binary to text conversion chart.

Some of you may be familiar with the ASCII conversion chart, and some of you may take one look at it and feel panic start to well up inside you. Before you start to panic, let's take a minute to break it down. You can start by thinking of it as a magic decoder ring. Take a look at the following string of binary digits.

```
01011001 01101111 01110101 01100011 01100001
01101110 01100100 01101111 01110100 01101000
01101001 01110011 00100001
```

Take the first eight digits: `01011001`. If you look at Table 1.1, you will find that this string translates or 'decodes' to the capital letter 'Y'. The

Table 1.1 *Binary/ASCII text/Hexadecimal conversion chart*

Binary	Glyph	HEX	Binary	Glyph	HEX	Binary	Glyph	HEX
00100000	(space)	20	01100000	`	60	01000000	@	40
00100001	!	21	01100001	a	61	01000001	A	41
00100010	"	22	01100010	b	62	01000010	B	42
00100011	#	23	01100011	c	63	01000011	C	43
00100100	$	24	01100100	d	64	01000100	D	44
00100101	%	25	01100101	e	65	01000101	E	45
00100110	&	26	01100110	f	66	01000110	F	46
00100111	'	27	01100111	g	67	01000111	G	47
00101000	(	28	01101000	h	68	01001000	H	48
00101001	)	29	01101001	i	69	01001001	I	49
00101010	*	2A	01101010	j	6A	01001010	J	4A
00101011	+	2B	01101011	k	6B	01001011	K	4B
00101100	,	2C	01101100	l	6C	01001100	L	4C
00101101	-	2D	01101101	m	6D	01001101	M	4D
00101110	.	2E	01101110	n	6E	01001110	N	4E
00101111	/	2F	01101111	o	6F	01001111	O	4F
00110000	0	30	01110000	p	70	01010000	P	50
00110001	1	31	01110001	q	71	01010001	Q	51
00110010	2	32	01110010	r	72	01010010	R	52
00110011	3	33	01110011	s	73	01010011	S	53
00110100	4	34	01110100	t	74	01010100	T	54
00110101	5	35	01110101	u	75	01010101	U	55
00110110	6	36	01110110	v	76	01010110	V	56
00110111	7	37	01110111	w	77	01010111	W	57
00111000	8	38	01111000	x	78	01011000	X	58
00111001	9	39	01111001	y	79	01011001	Y	59
00111010	:	3A	01111010	z	7A	01011010	Z	5A
00111011	;	3B	01111011	{	7B	01011011	[	5B
00111100	<	3C	01111100	|	7C	01011100	\	5C
00111101	=	3D	01111101	}	7D	01011101	]	5D
00111110	>	3E	01111110	~	7E	01011110	^	5E
00111111	?	3F				01011111	_	5F

second string of eight bits (`01101111`) maps to the letter 'o'. Going byte by byte, you can translate what would otherwise be a meaningless stream of zeros and ones into the meaningful sentence, 'You can do this!' You can also scan back up to the example of the binary information in the book arrangement and find that the books spell out the word, 'hi' in binary to ASCII encoding.

Not scary at all, right? In addition to ASCII, there are a number of other text encoding schemas. For example, the Unicode standard is used to encode nearly every written language into binary. ASCII has been included in the Unicode standard as a subset for the English language. Binary encoding can represent more than just the written word. It can also represent images, sound, video, databases and websites, each with their own general types of encoding, which are described through the rest of this chapter.

Hexadecimal

An intermediary form of digital encoding you should be familiar with is called hexadecimal. It shows up fairly often when analysing different aspects of born-digital content, so it is useful to be able to recognise it and understand the basics of how it works. The word 'hexadecimal' comes from the Greek, meaning 'sixteen', where 'hexa' means 'six' and 'decimal' means 'tenth'. Hexadecimal notation uses 16 characters represented by the numbers 0–9 and the letters A, B, C, D, E and F – as opposed to our usual decimal counting system, which uses a base of 10 characters (0–9).

You may have already encountered hexadecimal values if you have created a web page or have seen code that makes up a web page, since the colours for web pages are defined in hexadecimal values. For example, the code `#000000` represents black, `#ff000000` represents red and `#d49477` is a peachy taupe colour.

Hexadecimal can also be used to represent ASCII characters, as you may have noticed in Table 1.1. Using our example sentence, 'You can do this!', you can convert the ASCII text represented here into the following hexadecimal representation.

```
59 6F 75 20 63 61 6E 20 64 6F 20 74 68 69 73 21
```

You will learn more about viewing and interpreting files in hexadecimal in Chapter 3.

Digital file types

Let's take a brief look at some of the most common types of digital files. One of the great strengths of digital encoding is how a simple two-signal code (again, those 0s and 1s) can be variously encoded and schematised to present nearly anything. While you will be able to take a deep dive independently into any of the types covered here, we want to clarify at this point the basic processes and systems that allow 0s and 1s to move from text encoding to image display, audio playback and even relational databases. When you read this over, notice how digital encoding can move fluidly from objects with physical counterparts (e.g. images) to objects that are only ever digital (web pages).

Bitmapped images

Bitmapped images are one of the simplest types of digital image formats. A bitmapped image file has two main parts: the header and the image information. The header contains information that informs the computer of the file's format and provides information about the width, height and colour palette of the image. For example, the header for the example below would say that the image is 38 pixels wide, 25 pixels deep and that it uses a simple black and white colour palette. After this header information are the bits that will be used to represent the image. Look at the following string of binary information.

```
0000000000000000111111110000000000000000000000
0000011111111111111100000000000000000000011111
1111111111111100000000000000000111111111111111
1111111100000000000000111111111111111111111111
1000000000000111110000000001111111111111000000
0000111000000000000000000011111110000000011000
0000000000000000001111111000000011000000000000
0000000000000011110000011000000000000000000000
0000001111100001000000000000000000000000000000
1110001100000000000000000000000000000001110011
0000001100000000000000000000000111001100001111
1110000000000000000000001101110001101110110000
0000000000000000110110001111111111000000000000
0000000001011001111111101000000000000111110000
0101001111111000000000000000011111110001000111
0000000000000000000001011101100100000000000000
0000111111000111111110010000000000000000001111
1110001111111100000000000000000000011110100001
1111110000000000000000000000111110000000011100
0000000000000010000000000000000000110000000000
000000111111000000000000000100
```

Can you see the image? Probably not. But if we arrange this string of bits into the 38 x 25 bit grid, you might be able to see an image start to emerge:

```
00000000000000001111111100000000000000
00000000000001111111111111110000000000
00000000000111111111111111111100000000
00000000011111111111111111111111000000
00000000111111111111111111111111100000
00000001111100000000011111111111110000
00000011100000000000000000000111111100
00000110000000000000000000000111111100
00001100000000000000000000000000111100
00011000000000000000000000000000111110
00010000000000000000000000000000001110
00110000000000000000000000000000000111
00110000001100000000000000000000000111
00110000111111100000000000000000000011
01110001101110110000000000000000000011
01100011111111110000000000000000000001
01100111111110100000000000111110000001
01001111111000000000000000011111110001
00011100000000000000000000010111011001
00000000000000000011111100011111111001
00000000000000000011111110001111111100
00000000000000000001111010000111111100
00000000000000000000111111000000011100
00000000000000100000000000000000001100
00000000000000111111000000000000000100
```

When the appropriate software is used to open the image, the computer will follow the software's instructions to send a message to the monitor to represent each bit as coloured light. Since this is a simple black and white image, a 0 will be represented as a white block, and a 1 will be represented by a black block. Each block of colour is referred to as a pixel. If we translate each bit in the grid above into a black or white block, as we have in Figure 1.2 opposite, we can see the image of the adorable tree sloth as it was intended to appear on a computer screen.

Colour images are similar to black and white images, but are somewhat

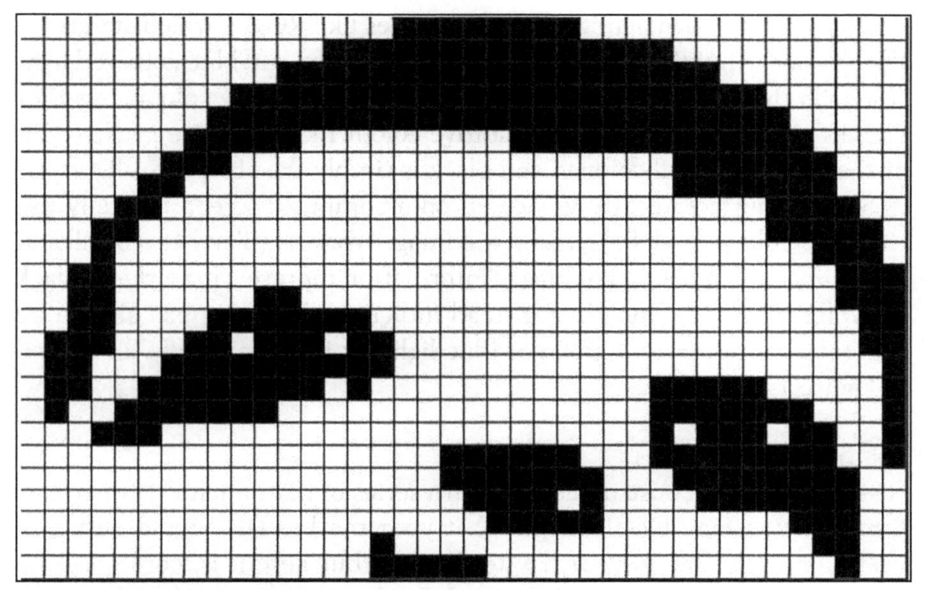

Figure 1.2 *Bitstream represented as a 15 pixel/inch bitmapped image*

more complicated. Instead of each pixel being displayed by one bit of information representing black or white, they are represented by longer strings of bits denoting colour. But how does digital colour work?

Everything we see is either light absorbing/reflecting or light emitting. Things like desks, images printed on paper, pianos and mountains absorb and reflect light. The colours we see when we look at these objects are the light spectrums that are reflected by the object, where all of the other spectrums of light are absorbed. The sun, light bulbs, TV screens and our computer monitors all emit light.

Anything that you create on your computer and print out is light absorbing/reflecting. When you are printing a document or image, you will print in black and white, greyscale or colour. Most colour printouts are printed in a 'colour model' called CMYK, which stands for the colours cyan, magenta, yellow, and the key to align the colours. We use the CMYK colour space for light absorbing/reflecting printed materials because it best represents the way colour works on printed materials. It is a subtractive colour model, meaning that you must remove or subtract colours to attain the colour white. When you layer cyan, magenta and yellow coloured ink on top of each other, the resulting colour is black. The colour white results from the absence of all colour.

Conversely, in light-emitting colour spaces like RGB – which stands for the colours red, green and blue – layering red, green and blue coloured light results in the colour white. The fact that adding all of the colours together creates white light makes it an additive colour model. White is the result of the presence of all colours, and black is simply the absence of light.

Still images created to be viewed on a computer screen typically use the RGB colour model. A colour still image works similarly to a black and white image, but instead of binary information representing either a black or white pixel, the encoding instead indicates that the pixel should be presented as either red, green or blue light, as in the example illustrated in Figure 1.3.

Vector and 3D images

A vector image is constructed through a series of mathematical equations. Some of you may have thought that your maths class would never be useful or applicable in your day-to-day life, but here it is, come back to haunt you. But please don't worry. Whether you received high or low marks in maths, it's a pretty easy concept to grasp here; I promise, you won't have to calculate the area of any complex shapes.

Simply put, a vector image is made up of mathematical information

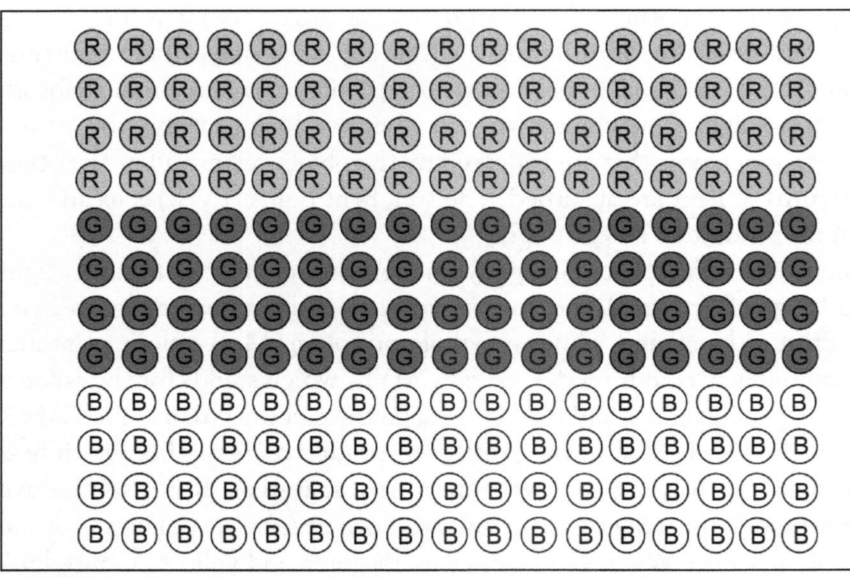

Figure 1.3 *Pixels encoded in the Red (R), Green (G), and Blue (B) colour space, used in both still images and what would be a single frame in a digital video*

that describes starting points, ending points, angles, curves and fill colours and styles. Figure 1.4 shows a simple, curved line comprised of a starting point, an endpoint and two bars that are used to set the curve of the line, or the Bézier curve. This curve was named for Pierre Bézier, the French engineer who developed the method for mathematically defining smooth curves, which was commonly used in the automobile industry. Bézier curves are the backbone for all vector images and shape-drawing software. We see our friend, the sloth, again in Figure 1.5 (on the next page) as a vector graphic. You can see that her lines are much smoother and clearer than in the low-resolution bitmapped version in Figure 1.2.

The instructions for creating the image are encoded as a text, like ASCII described above. In this case, the text is encoded in the UTF-8 (Unicode Transformation Format-8) character encoding, which is part of the Unicode standard. The software used to render the image decodes the binary information back into text and then uses the text instructions to construct the image.

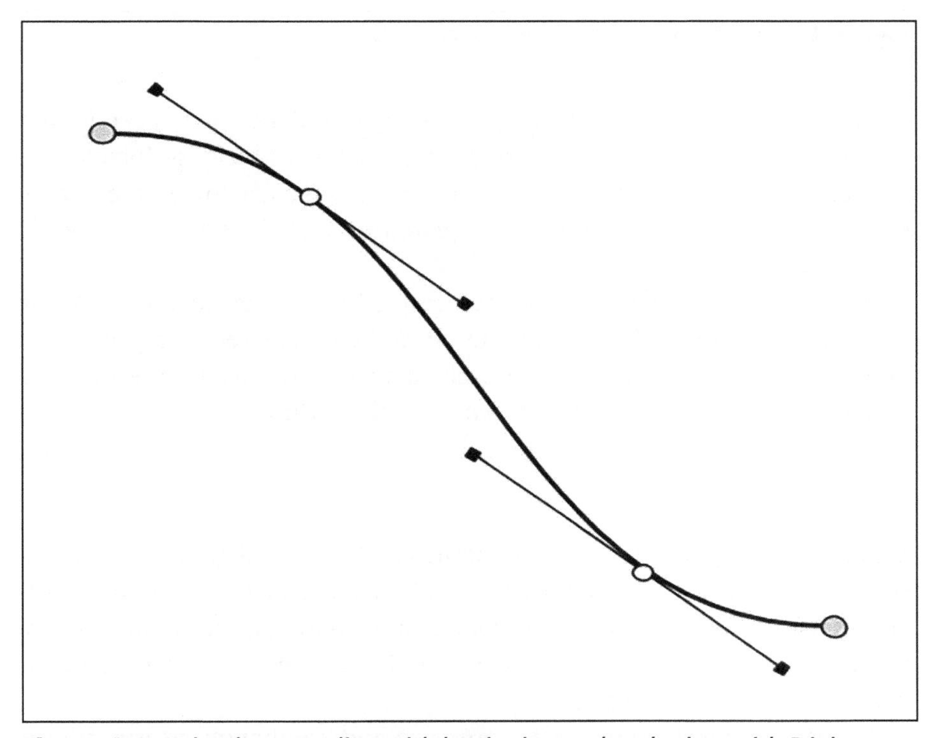

Figure 1.4 *A simple vector line with beginning and endpoints with Bézier curve adjusters*

Figure 1.5 *Our friend, the sloth, as a vector graphic*

A big difference between bitmapped images and vector images is that when you enlarge a bitmapped image it can appear blocky or 'pixelated'. Because the shape in a vector image file is defined solely by mathematical equations, you can scale a one inch square image to the size of a billboard with no loss of image quality.

3D images are similar to 2D vector images in that they are created using geometric equations. Instead of the image being created using only two points of reference (e.g. two dimensions on x- and y-axes), the image is created using three points of reference, or three dimensions on x-, y- and z-axes.

Audio files

What we experience as sound are actually vibrations that create physical waves of varying pressure and frequency. Our ears pick up the sound waves and transmit the pressure and frequency information to our brains, where we perceive it as sound. Capturing and recording sound to tape or computer works similarly.

To record sound, sound wave pressure and frequency information is captured through a microphone. This information can be stored as either continuous analogue information or sampled digital information. In sampled digital information, the entire soundwave is not captured, but rather only periodic samples of the wave. The more frequent the sample rate of the soundwave, the truer the digital recording is to the original sound that was recorded. The process of representing samples of an analogue sound wave as digital information is called pulse-code modulation. Figure 1.6 illustrates various sampling moments on a sound wave. The information about their location on the wave is then encoded into binary form, which can then be transformed back into sound by a digital signal processor.

Video files

Video files are made up of both visual and audio information. Generally speaking, a video file acts more like a container that contains both video and audio information together. You may have heard the terms 'codec' and 'container' in discussions about video file formats. These terms refer to slightly different things, but are sometimes used interchangeably. To describe it simply, a codec is the set of rules that describes how the file

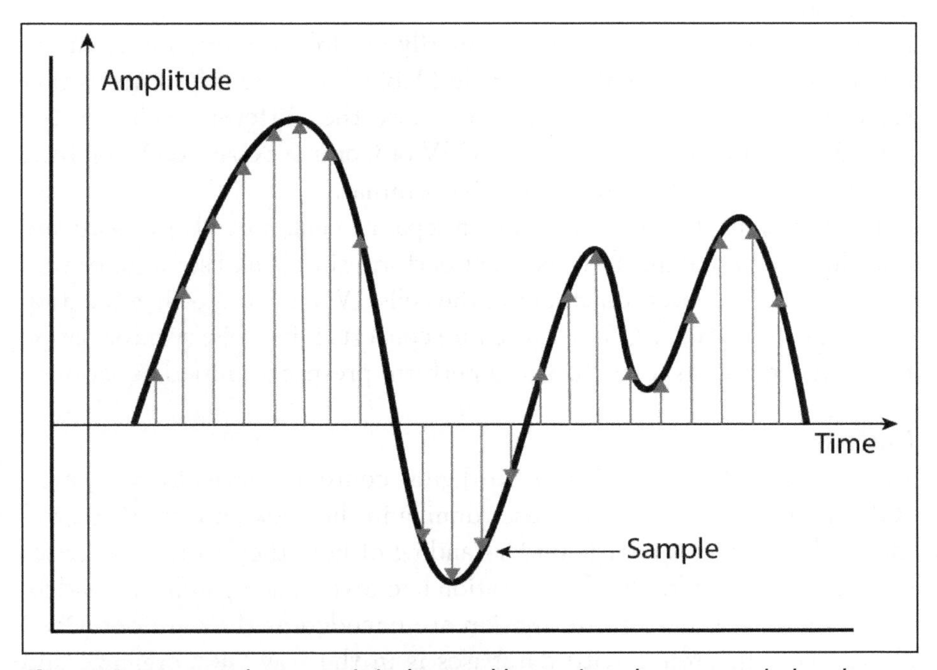

Figure 1.6 *A sound wave as it is detected by a microphone, sampled and translated into digital information*

should be encoded and decoded. A container, often called the file format, holds a group of video, audio and other related files together. The audio information is encoded as described above and illustrated in Figure 1.5 and packaged with the video file in a container format.

You can think of the video information as being thousands of images recorded and presented one after the other in quick succession. These images are commonly referred to as frames, and the number of frames per second (fps) is called the frame rate. A common frame rate is 24fps, or 24p. A typical two-hour movie filmed at 24p will have 172,800 frames; that's a lot of images!

A majority of contemporary moving image frames use a colour space based on RGB called YCbCr. The Y represents the luminosity of the pixel, meaning how bright or dark it is. Cb represents the 'blue-difference' or where on the blue to yellow scale it is. Cr represents the 'red-difference' or where on the red to green scale it is. Each of the 172,800 frames of a two-hour movie will be encoded similarly to the RGB image illustrated in Figure 1.3, but using YCbCr or various other colour space encoding.

Spreadsheets

A basic spreadsheet is encoded primarily as alphanumeric information, much like text in the ASCII example (Table 1.1). The difference is that separator characters are added to mark the different cells in the spreadsheet. You may have heard of CSV or Comma Separated Value files, where the cells of data are marked by commas.

In addition to storing information in separate cells, spreadsheet software also allows you to enter formulas that perform simple and sometimes very complex mathematical equations in the cells. When you type in a function name like 'SUM' or 'COS' the software converts it into binary information that it recognises as instructions to perform pre-programmed equations.

Databases

Almost every library and archive digital content management system (CMS) has some sort of database running in the back end, so it's a good idea to have at least a basic understanding of how they work. Databases can store different kinds of information like text, images, audio and video. The individual types of information are encoded as they are described above. The difference with databases is in the way they organize and retrieve the information they store. Most databases work by using a system of tables to organize their data. The most common of these is the relational database.

Databases organize their information similarly to spreadsheets, by collecting and arranging the information in cells under particular headings. Information is collected and arranged like this across several (sometimes even hundreds) of tables, and relationships are formed across the tables via shared 'key fields'. For example, you might have a 'CreatorData' table listing creator names, a number associated with each creator, where they work and a number associated with their favourite animal. You could have another table called 'Videos' that has titles of videos, video file formats, creation dates for the videos and creator numbers. You could have a third table that has a column for animal numbers, names of animals, the animals' favourite foods and the numbers associated with the creators who love them. As you can see in Figure 1.7, the three tables can be connected via the key field, 'CreatorNum'. The 'CreatorData' and 'Animals' tables can be connected via the 'FavAnimalNum' field. The connecting 'relationships'

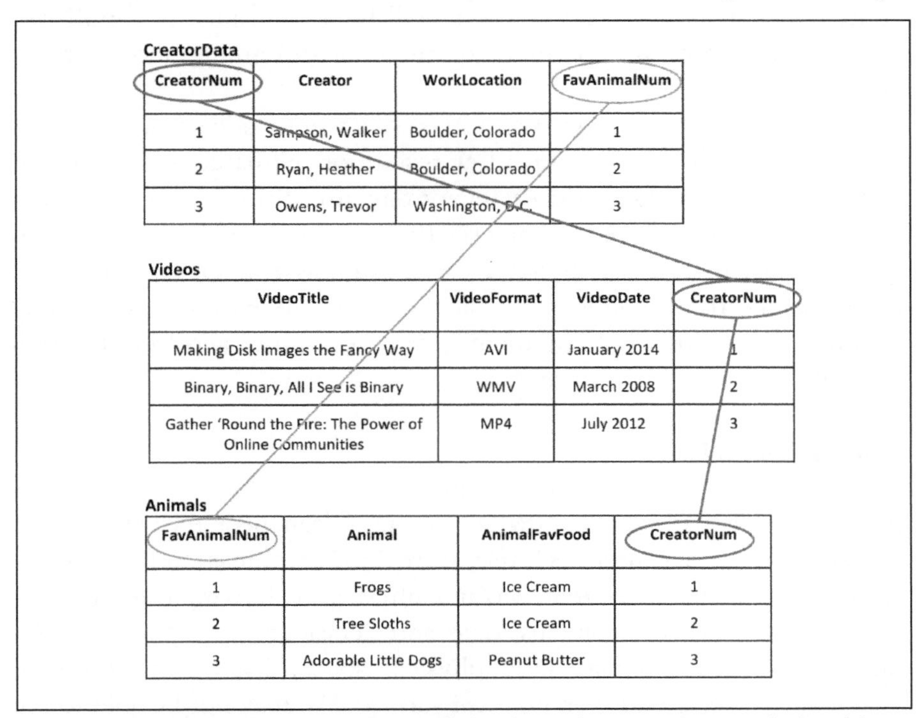

CreatorData

CreatorNum	Creator	WorkLocation	FavAnimalNum
1	Sampson, Walker	Boulder, Colorado	1
2	Ryan, Heather	Boulder, Colorado	2
3	Owens, Trevor	Washington, D.C.	3

Videos

VideoTitle	VideoFormat	VideoDate	CreatorNum
Making Disk Images the Fancy Way	AVI	January 2014	1
Binary, Binary, All I See is Binary	WMV	March 2008	2
Gather 'Round the Fire: The Power of Online Communities	MP4	July 2012	3

Animals

FavAnimalNum	Animal	AnimalFavFood	CreatorNum
1	Frogs	Ice Cream	1
2	Tree Sloths	Ice Cream	2
3	Adorable Little Dogs	Peanut Butter	3

Figure 1.7 *Three tables in a relational database showing the 21 relationships between the Favourite Animal (FavAnimalNum) and Creator rNum) fields between the tables*

of the 'CreatorNum' and 'FavAnimalNum' fields is where the name 'relational database' originates.

Web pages

At their heart, web pages are essentially text files that web browsers translate into what you see on your screen. Looking at it more closely, they are somewhat more complicated. In most cases, what you see when you are viewing a web page is actually a conglomeration of every type of digital information we have discussed so far. You will see or hear text, images, audio and video; and all of this is most likely served up to you through a back-end database.

The core of web page construction is the HyperText Markup Language, or HTML. The HTML language defines standardised ways to describe how a web page will look and behave. In addition to HTML, web pages can be constructed using other languages like JavaScript, Cascading Style Sheets, PHP, Java, Python and Ruby. As your knowledge of born-digital content becomes more advanced, it will be a good idea to familiarise yourself with how one or more of these programming and scripting languages work.

In the mid-1990s most web pages you saw were made up of static text and images, with the occasional low-resolution animated gif. You could return to the web page address every day, use different computers in different geographic locations, and see the same content. Today web pages are substantially more complex and are often assembled from bits and pieces on the fly whenever you visit the page. The page can be entirely different from moment to moment, from user to user and from location to location.

Storage media

I'd like to point out a potentially dangerous and confusing fallacy that is prevalent in discussions about digital content. Often, people will talk about digital and physical content as if they were different things, and specifically speaking as if digital content was not physical. Following this mode of thought can lead to erroneous ideas and decisions down the road. All digital information exists in a physical space. Every bit of digital information is encoded on a physical surface. We may not be able to see the marks or signals with the naked eye, but they are marked somewhere, just as ink on paper. Understanding this may be a good first step in demystifying digital content. The less we think about digitally encoded information as something magical floating in the ether, the more we can grasp what we need to do to preserve and provide access to it over time.

How are physical marks of digital information made and recorded, if not magically? Three of the most common methods of physically recording digital information are on magnetic media, optical media and solid-state media.

Magnetic media

Binary information is recorded onto magnetic media by using – you guessed it – a magnet. Magnetic media's ink, so to speak, is a thin layer of iron oxide, and its paper is a thin disk of plastic. The read-write head used to 'write' information to the disk contains a tiny iron core, wrapped with a thin coil of wire. When an electric current is sent through the coil of wire, the iron core becomes an electromagnet that can magnetise the particles in the disk's iron oxide coating.

As the electromagnetic head passes over the iron oxide particles, it changes the position of their magnetic poles. The direction of the poles is set at either north or south, depending on the direction of the electric current passing through the coil of wire. Each bit of information is made up of two bands of particles. In the first band, the particles are aligned in one direction. If the second band of particles is aligned in the same direction as the first band, this bit will be read as a binary 0. If the second band is aligned in the opposite direction as the first band, it will be read as a binary 1. The band following any complete bit is always aligned in the opposite polar direction of the band before it to indicate the presence of a new bit.

Binary information is stored as a series of magnetised fluxes in one of two opposite directions, and the difference in polarity of the magnetised material can be detected and read back into the system through the read-and-write head. The magnetisation of the material is persistent (barring the inevitable degradation of a magnetised field, and the magnetised materials, over time) after the oxide side has been read or written to. This is why you can turn your computer off after writing a file to the disk and still have that data when you turn the system back on: your magnetic storage is *non-volatile* – it does not need a constant current through it to retain data (you do, of course, need a current to perform reads and writes!). Floppy disks, hard disks, cassette tapes, the once-dominant VHS video tapes, reel-to-reel tape and the majority of the hard drives on the market store information in this way.

Recording binary information to a disk is just the first step in encoding and decoding meaningful information on magnetic media. Magnetic disks are typically formatted in different ways, depending on the type of computer system used to write to the disk. The type of formatting used is called the file system. One common file system used on disks is the File Allocation Table (FAT) file system. In a FAT file system, the disk is divided into sections called sectors and clusters. The outermost ring of sectors contains the FAT that stores all of the information about which files are written to the disk and where they are written.

When you click 'Save' in a file you are working on, the computer searches the FAT for unallocated sectors, meaning sectors to which no file information has been assigned. The system will then assign segments of the file to different unallocated sectors of the disk. The disk locations of the file segments are recorded in the FAT and the file is written to the disk. Reading the file back involves the system looking up the file's segment locations in the FAT, pulling the segments together and then feeding them to the software you are using to read it. Depending on the file system (and version of that file system) used by your operating system, there are other intermediary processes, but this gives you a good idea of the core function and importance of the file system – it is a fundamental organizing layer between the signals read from and written to the storage device to the actual files that an operating system uses. Different filing systems were developed for magnetic tape media, like IBM's Linear Tape File System (LTFS), and some file systems can be adjusted to work with newer media (such as FAT32 working with solid-state drives). We will talk about file systems more and how they impact on your work in Chapter 3.

Optical media

Optical media, like CDs, CD-ROMs, DVDs and Blu-ray disks store microscopic binary information on a flat disk, much like magnetic disks, but use very different methods to do so. Instead of iron oxide, the 'ink' in this case is made up of a reflective layer (sometimes made of gold) and a layer of a specially formulated chemical that reacts to laser light.

The writing and reading process is different still between rewritable and non-rewritable disks. When writing information to non-rewritable disks, a laser will strike areas on the disk which will cause the area to form a small bubble or dome. When the disk is read in an optical disk drive, a laser in the read head will shine its light onto the disk. When the laser strikes areas that have a bubble, the light will be refracted away from the sensor in the head. In this case, no information is received and the space on the disk is recorded as a 0. When the laser strikes an area that has no bubble, the light will pass through the surface of the disk to the reflective layer, and will be reflected back to the read head sensor. When this happens, the signal is recorded as a 1.

In the case of rewritable optical disks, both the read-and-write laser and the reactive chemical are different. First, the read-and-write head laser is designed to produce laser light at two different temperatures. Second, the chemical substrate is designed to be clear when struck by one temperature of laser, and opaque when struck by the other temperature. The substrate can be struck by the laser again and be changed to either clear or opaque, thus allowing the binary information recorded on the disk to be changed.

Reading the information off the disk is similar to reading a non-rewritable disk. When the laser hits the opaque areas of the disk, no light is reflected back and therefore no signal received, resulting in the read of a binary 0. When the light strikes a clear area, it will strike the reflective surface underneath and be reflected back to the sensor, resulting in the read of a binary 1.

Unlike magnetic disks, optical disks are not broken into radiating sectors, but rather their data are arranged in one long spiral. Consequently, their file systems are designed to reflect this difference. Common file systems for optical storage media are ISO 9660 and the Universal Disk Format.

Solid-state storage

Solid-state storage is often referred to as a solid-state drive or a solid-state disk, even though it contains neither a disk nor a moving drive to spin a disk. As its name implies, it has no discernibly moving parts. Beyond external and internal solid state ‘drives’, you can find solid state storage in your smartphone, SD cards for digital camera and USB or flash drives.

Solid-state storage is similar to magnetic media in that it uses electricity to create the different states to be written and recorded as binary information. The process to write and read solid-state data is, however, somewhat more complicated. Reduced to its simplest form, solid-state storage writes and reads binary information by using pulses of different voltages of electricity to push electrons into what is called a 'control gate', where they are trapped. In this system, transistors that have no charge are read as a 1 and transistors that have a negative charge are read as a 0. From this you can deduce that transistors that are filled with trapped electrons will have a negative charge, and therefore be read as a 0.

Solid-state storage uses file systems that are similar to magnetic and optical media, but they are typically optimised for the different read-and-write environment of solid-state. In particular, data cells in solid-state storage can wear out quickly if they are rewritten too many times. Some file systems have been designed to minimise the wear by ensuring that cells are rewritten equally across the storage device in a process is called 'wear levelling'.

Command line basics

A number of tools and methods that you will use to process and manage born-digital content involve using a command line interface. A command line interface is a way of interacting with a computer using text-based prompts instead of the familiar graphical user interface (GUI – pronounced 'gooey') where you can point and click on icons, buttons and menus to perform actions. The command line interface hails from the early days of computing where the only way to perform actions on a computer, such as opening files or running a script or program, was to type out specific commands in a simple text interface. Even though almost all human–computer interaction today is supported by nearly seamless GUIs, we can still navigate and control our computers through the 'old school' command line interface. This works a little differently for personal computers (PCs) and Apple Macs, so I will go over some basic principles for each.

Before doing so, I want to demystify the command line a little. I'm sure that some of you are very familiar with the command line and have no trepidation about using it. Some of you may have an image in your mind of coding and hacker geniuses tapping away on their keyboards at lightning speed, performing magical feats via the command line. You may think that you don't fit that image at all and that you could never be one of the super geniuses that use command line to control their computers. If this is you, I would take you gently by the shoulders, look you in the eye and tell you that it's not nearly as complicated as you might think. That's not to say that command line is the easiest or most intuitive thing to figure out. Some of the commands are obscure and don't make a lot of sense. It's really a matter of diving in and familiarising yourself with the commands, how they work and what they can do for you. It just takes time, patience and perseverance. You can do this! And I'm going to show you how.

At the time of writing, on most Windows machines you can access a command line interface by launching 'Command Prompt' under 'Programs', or simply typing 'cmd' (for command line) into the Run prompt available on the Start menu. (On Windows 10, type 'cmd' into the search box and the Command Prompt program will appear in the search results.) On a Mac, you can access the command line using the 'Terminal' program in the Utilities folder.

Once you have access to a command line type the following and hit Enter:

```
ls (for Mac/Linux)
dir (for PC)
```

This will present you with a list of all of the files and directories (also known as folders) in your current location. You can change directories by typing 'cd' and the name of whichever directory you would like to enter. One of my favourite shortcuts is typing the first letter of the directory I want to enter, and then hitting the Tab key. If there are no other directories that begin with the same letter, the terminal will automatically type out the rest of the directory name. Once you hit 'Enter', you can enter 'ls' (Mac/Linux) or 'dir' (PC) again to see a list of files and directories in your new location.

You can create a new directory by using the 'mkdir' command followed by the name you would like to assign the new directory. Take a minute to try this, and then navigate through your GUI interface to where you created the folder. There it is! I know this may be a small victory, but the first time I created a directory through the command line I felt pretty proud of myself.

There are a couple of ways you can create new files using the command line. One is by using the **vi** or **Vim** editor, and another is using the **Emacs** editor. Just as there are Mac and PC camps, there are also impassioned supporters of Vim and Emacs. Do feel free to use whichever editor works best for you. Choosing either does not necessarily put you in the middle of the 'editor war'.

In the Unix or Apple environment, you can open Vim by simply typing 'vim' and either the name of an existing file or the name you would like to assign to a new file. PCs don't come loaded with vi or Vim in the default Windows install, so if you are working on a PC you will have to download and install the software first – visit vim.org to do so. Once it is installed and running, you will be presented with a clear screen in which you can type out your desired content. Because you are still in a command line interface, you will need to use specific commands to perform actions while in the Vim document.

Unlike working in a GUI text interface (like Microsoft Word), you can't immediately start editing your document as soon as it's open. You must first change to editing mode by typing 'i' to insert text at the cursor. You can use the arrow keys to navigate to different locations in the text. There are several other commands you can use to insert or edit text throughout your document, which you can find online. It takes a little bit of time to become accustomed to writing and editing in Vim and Emacs but, with practice, it eventually becomes like second nature.

Once you have finished editing your document, you can save your work and quit Vim by typing ':x' or ':wq'. You can also type ':q', but your changes may not necessarily be saved. To explicitly quit Vim without saving your changes, you can type ':q!'. Now you can hop over to your GUI interface, find the file you just created, and open it up in your favourite GUI text software to see your new creation in a more familiar environment.

You may also need to upload and download files from remote servers using the File Transfer Protocol (FTP). For this you will need to know the location of the files, your username and password. A search online will bring up any number of other command line resources that will be useful as well.

Code repositories

A great deal of the software and code snippets you may use to manage your born-digital content are available in code repositories like GitHub and Sourceforge. At first glance, visiting these repositories may feel like you've just entered a foreign country. Don't worry, a lot of people have that same reaction, but before long you will feel right at home. Who knows, you may even start creating and uploading your own software in one of these code repositories!

Most of the software I've run across in this field I've found on GitHub, so I'll focus there. Often, you'll find your way to a GitHub page either through an online search or from a link on someone's website. When you get to the code page, you will discover, probably to your dismay, a page with a list of very obscure and confusingly named files. If you just want to download and install the code, you can usually find a button somewhere on the page marked 'download' or 'clone or download'.

Typically, clicking this button will give you an option to download some sort of code package which you can download, open and use from there. It's usually a good idea to take a look at any available `README.txt` files shared on the page as well as any installation guides provided. There will usually be a link to an external web page that may provide more information about how to install and use the software, and it's a good idea to follow the link and read whatever information is available there. Some tools and software packages have more guidance and documentation than others. If you find yourself in a situation where you know you need a particular tool, but the site has little helpful documentation, you can always seek out help from others via listservs, online groups or social media channels.

Conclusion

Congratulations! You've just made it through a very technologically dense chapter. We assure you that understanding the basics of how digital information works is going to be a very valuable tool for you as you make decisions and write policies for acquiring, processing, describing, preserving and providing access to born-digital content. The rest of this book is built on the foundation of this knowledge. These concepts will be built on in more detail and depth and will be covered in the context of workflows, policy and real-life use cases. After reading this chapter you should know:

- What digital information is and how it is encoded and translated into meaningful signals
- How information is encoded on and retrieved from various digital storage media
- Some basics of using a command line interface to interact with computers
- A little bit about code repositories and how they may be useful to you.

Further reading

Robbins, A. (2006) *Unix in a Nutshell*, 4th edn, O'Reilly Media, Inc.

A great desk reference for command line prompts. Not exactly a page-turner, but an invaluable, in-depth resource for commands and all of their variations. Includes Unix commands, some regular expressions, Emacs, vi and vim commands as well as short chapters on other various tools that you may find handy.

White, A. (2014) *How Computers Work*, 10th edn, Que Publishing.

A fantastic introduction to the basics of computers and how they function. The entire book is comprised of colour illustrations and easy-to-understand descriptions.

CHAPTER 2

Selection

> No history can be a faithful mirror. If it were, it would be as long and as dull as life itself. It must be a selection, and, being a selection, must inevitably be biased. (T. E. Hulme, 1911)

Selecting the material your institution will steward, perhaps indefinitely, is probably the most important step in managing born-digital content. It is from these decisions that all other things will follow. Luckily, there are decades of theory and practice around collection development and archival appraisal that can guide your own selection decisions. In this chapter, we review the various types of born-digital content you may acquire; different factors that may influence your collecting decisions; and approaches for developing a mission- and policy-driven collecting strategy. We also take a look at an approach for expanding traditional gift agreements to include born-digital content, and explore Stanford University's guidance for selection procedures for web archiving.

Types of born-digital content

Because born-digital content is any record or information that was created in digital form, it can come to libraries and archives in a number of ways and in various formats. When it comes to deciding which content to collect, born-digital content is not all that different from paper-based content. There are a few differences you should consider, however.

First, you have to keep in mind that digital content will require a greater commitment of time and resources to preserve and provide access to over time. In most cases, it will require you to establish a new or improved technological infrastructure to host the content. If your institution is already invested in managing digital content and you already have strong relationships established with those who manage your technological infrastructure and storage, this could be relatively simple. Often, however, this can involve establishing new relationships with information technology (IT) managers and negotiating for their time, expertise and other resources to be allocated to managing your digital content.

What all of this boils down to is that your institution's ability to commit to the long-term preservation and access of born-digital content strongly affects your appraisal and selection of that content. While some guidelines for collecting decisions state that format should not have a bearing on appraisal and collection, you and your institution's preparedness to manage and protect born-digital content may affect your decision to collect it.

Let's take a look at the different types of born-digital content that can come under the purview of libraries and archives. Take a second to think about all of the different types of digital information you create and encounter every day. Our lives have evolved to a point where almost everything we do occurs through one sort of digital channel or another, between our computers, our mobile phones and even things like our cars, refrigerators and toasters. Not all of these digital channels result in the creation of records that we would want to save and provide access to in the future, but quite a few of them do. Of these, just about any of them can find their way into a library or archives and fall under your care.

The list of possible types of digital information that libraries and archives can and should steward grows year by year. We can no longer stay in our comfort zone of managing only digital documents and images which are dealt with more easily due to the similarities they feature with their physical counterparts. Let's take a look at some of the types of digital information you might find yourself considering for acquisition.

- **3D** modelling, animation and rendering software is becoming more ubiquitous and is becoming an increasingly important vehicle for expression and documentation. 3D modelling is often used to document historic places and artefacts that exist in analogue spaces; but it is also used to create digital-only artefacts and spaces such as those found in online virtual worlds like Second Life, virtual video game spaces like Minecraft and World of Warcraft, many contemporary video games and the growing 3D video creation market, which includes purely artistic or expressive works. These types of digital 3D creations can constitute vital documentation of our life, society and culture that libraries and archives should collect and preserve over time.

- Almost all **audio** recordings created today are produced in digital form. Digital audio content can contain important musical creations, recordings of lectures, presentations, podcasts, spoken word performances, documentation of historical events, records of human rights violations and more. Having an understanding of and strategy to collect and manage digital audio content is a must.
- If you look at the back end of almost any content management or online communication system, you will find that they are all driven by **relational databases**. The data collected and displayed by social media sites (Facebook, Twitter, Snapchat), CMSs (DSpace, Drupal, WordPress), news sites (New York Times, BBC, Huffington Post) and journal subscription services (JSTOR, EBSCO, ProQuest) all use some type of relational database on the back end. The most common types of relational databases are those designed for the Structured Query Language (SQL), often referred to as SQL databases. Beyond SQL, there are dozens of other types of relational database frameworks, both current and legacy, that contain valuable data and that you might have to consider collecting. All of this data and the databases themselves are born-digital content that can be valuable enough to collect, manage and provide access to in your library or archive.
- Digital **documents** in the form of Microsoft Word files and Portable Document Format (PDF) files have long been common formats managed by libraries and archives. Their ubiquity in library and archive repositories has given rise to the relative ease with which they can be managed, and is proof positive that these documents contain information that is valuable enough to collect.
- At this point, books are almost always drafted digitally in one word processor another. To the extent that you are interested in collecting drafts of published or unpublished works, you will be acquiring and managing born-digital materials. Should a work be published, it is often published as an **e-book** – a completely digital copy. In some cases, a finished work is published *only* as an e-book. Regardless, books, whether paper or digital, have great value to libraries and their user services. Managing e-books can be complicated by the fact that they are often distributed through vendors who control the function, look and feel of the access system, and who can place various restrictions on access, printing and downloading the content. In these

cases, managing e-books becomes more a function of managing your relationship with the vendor and negotiating contracts that best suit the needs of your institution and its patrons.

- Similar to e-books, **electronic journals** are an electronic representation of what had previously been experienced as printed journals. Like e-books, the challenge of managing electronic journals often lies in the relationship and contracts with the vendors who supply access to the journals.
- Originally designed as a method to electronically send and deliver messages to distant (and sometimes nearby) individuals, **e-mail** has become a dominant means of communication for those with access to the internet. Letters between individuals have long been acquired by archives for their research and evidentiary value (discussed in more detail below), so it should be no surprise that e-mail can be just as valuable in archives that collect born-digital content.
- Like documents, digital **images** are one of the more common type of content found in digital repositories. Similarly, their ubiquity has given rise to established best practices for their management and long-term care. Digital images serve the same role as photographs in collections, and so are historically known to have a high potential for carrying valuable information that should be collected and preserved.
- **Linked data** is an increasingly important method for creating connections between various information sources and the contents therein; these connections can be read by people and automatically processed by computers. It may be important for your institution to monitor and preserve the functionality of documents that contain linked data and include it in your collecting purview.
- Similarly, **metadata**, though not the primary information source, is important to consider in collection management, and these days is almost always born digital. Without the metadata that describes them, much of the value of our collections is diminished or even completely destroyed.
- If you think about how you and people you know create and send the most information, you may come to realise that most of the modern world's information exchange happens via mobile phones, smartphones or some type of **mobile device** (such as PDAs – personal digital assistants – or tablets). These days, mobile devices are designed like computers and can contain the same types of files as

computers such as e-mail, photos, contacts, calendars, web browsing data, PDFs, etc. They can also contain SMS (short message service) and MMS (multimedia messaging service) messages, location information and messages and data collected using any number of apps. Any of this type of information could be considered for collecting.

- Similarly, collecting **feed lists** and **playlists** (RSS, Spotify, Soundcloud, etc.) could add great contextual information to a collection, particularly those highlighting artists, writers, musicians or other creatives. It may also be useful to know what articles a scientist was reading or what music they were listening to when they were developing Nobel Prize-winning work.
- Where lives of the past were documented primarily through records, journals, letters, and photographs, the lives of today are documented and shared predominantly through **social media** hubs like Facebook, Twitter, Snapchat, YouTube and Instagram. It is certainly worth our time to find strategies for collecting and preserving this form of information. We will touch on acquisition considerations for these types of services in Chapter 3.
- While it is generally not considered to contain the content that libraries and archives collect, the **software** used to create and provide access to digital content is certainly worthwhile to collect and preserve. Groups like the Software Preservation Network focus on bringing community partners together to tackle the greater issues of preserving software. We will talk about software as a preservation object a little more in Chapter 8.
- **Spreadsheets** with various types of data (geospatial, medical, astronomical, genetic, humanities and other various quantitative and qualitative data) are a ubiquitous source of valuable information that you may want to collect. You may have the opportunity to collect spreadsheet files in VisiCalc from the late 1970s, simple CSV files or more complex contemporary files with visualisations and embedded macros.
- **Video** files are another common file type that is becoming a staple in library and archives collections. With the rise of easy digital video capture devices and faster internet upload and streaming speeds, video is quickly becoming a dominant documentation format today.
- There are active and passionate communities devoted to collecting and preserving **computer and video games**. Whether or not your

institution is interested in collecting these cultural artefacts, it's a good idea to be aware of these dedicated groups and enthusiasts, as they have developed a number of processes and tools that library and archives institutions have adopted in their broader born-digital collection management workflows.

- Related to video games, **virtual spaces** can provide great research value, but also pose some interesting challenges for collection and preservation over time. Consider shared or solitary virtual spaces such as those created in Second Life and Minecraft, as well as online group game spaces such as massively multiplayer online role-playing games and their predecessor, multi-user dungeon games.
- As data **visualisation** is becoming more popular you may also be presented with opportunities to collect the outputs and original files and code used to create visualised data. Keep in mind that static visualisations such as charts and diagrams can be as simple as collecting images, but more complex animated and time-based visualisations will require deeper consideration of the tools and resources required to maintain their functionality.
- **Websites** are also proving to be an important information source to collect and preserve. You may consider collecting and preserving your own institution's web pages as well as others that fit within your collection policies.

Ultimately, decisions on selecting content for your library or archives will depend on whether or not the material fits your institution's mission. In most cases, the processes of appraising or selecting are very similar to those for paper-based content. There are some cases, however, where you may have to consider format, media and size in your collecting decisions.

Format- versus content-driven collecting decisions

Each of the types of digital information listed above can present its own unique opportunity or challenge when you are making collection development and appraisal decisions. In many cases, especially for formats that are common and which have known handling procedures, there will be little-to-no barrier to acquiring certain material. Other formats and particularly large digital objects and collections may pose some difficult or even insurmountable challenges.

Particularly in the earlier days of digital content collecting, certain institutions limited what they would collect based on the formats they knew they could manage. If you have confidence in your ability to preserve and provide long-term access to only certain file formats, it is perfectly reasonable to shape your collecting policies around this.

You may, however, be in a situation where you cannot exclude relevant content based on format, media or size. This is the case in many state and government archives in the USA, where legal requirements compel collection and preservation of the records of related government agencies 'for the life of the republic' – regardless of the format, media or size. This is also the case for government libraries and archives across the globe. For example, Archives New Zealand is faced with this same mandate and has begun work on tackling born-digital content under the auspices of the Interim Response to Born-Digital Records in Archives. In such cases the appraisal and collecting decisions are less about the capacity to manage and preserve content in different digital formats and more about the content produced by the related government units. Looking at this more broadly, content-driven collecting decisions should be aligned to your institution's collecting mission and can be guided little, or not at all, by format requirements.

Mission statements, collection policies and donor agreements

Mission statements, collection policies and donor agreements all play an important role in guiding the process of selecting and acquiring born-digital content. Mission statements provide the overarching shape of the collecting areas and help to determine what types of content can be acquired in your institution. They feed into the collection policies, which provide more specific guidance about the content and formats your institution is willing to acquire. Donor agreements flow from your mission statements and collection policies in that they outline how this guidance is actualised in a gift or transfer of resources.

Mission statements

As with all types of content, deciding what born-digital content to collect comes down to whether or not the content satisfies your collecting mission. The best first step for ensuring that born-digital content is something your institution can take on is to take a look at your mission statement. Most mission statements are broad enough to include born-digital content, but some may need some adjustments to do so. If you don't have a mission statement, creating one is a good first step for defining the type of content you collect.

Here, we provide you with a number of examples of mission statements from various institutions that can help you better shape your existing mission statement, or help you create a new one.

General mission statements

The following mission statements are good examples of missions that provide a general outline of their goals, very broad statements of whom they serve and what informational resources they may steward. Both of these examples are very succinct, yet serve as a broad net that provides the necessary guidance for forming more specific collection policies. When reading through these, consider how these mission statements might be used to create a more defined collection policy.

The mission of the National Archives of Japan is: 'To contribute to the development of democracy and the realisation of a high quality of life through the preservation and use of public archives as shared assets of the people.' The Archives' purpose as described here is to, 'contribute to the development of democracy and the realisation of a high quality of life'. The mission statement very gently refers to the 'public archives' as the content of the Archives, and it references 'the people' as the intended user of the Archives. While this mission statement doesn't mention any specific format, it is broad enough to include any type of content, including born-digital.

In contrast, the mission of the Forestry Research Institute of Ghana Library has much more specific language about the type of resources it collects. Its mission is: 'to build a comprehensive collection of recorded information on forestry and forest related disciplines, and to make its resources available and useful to students, lecturers, scientists and the general public. It is also aimed at ensuring that these resources are sustained and preserved for future generations.' Like the National Archives of Japan's mission statement, this statement has no specific reference to format, which leaves room for incorporating born-digital content into collection policies.

Mission statements specific to digital

While it can be a good idea to leave your mission statements broad enough to encompass a variety of formats, there are some cases where it is better to explicitly include reference to digital content. It is important to include reference to digital material in your mission statement if your primary function is that of a digital library or archives, but it can also be relevant to include if you know your audience has a demonstrated need for the content in digital form. This being said, it is rare to find mission statements that include reference to digital content, and even more rare that they highlight born-digital content – highlighted by the fact that we were not able to locate mission statements referencing born-digital content at the time of writing. That's not to say that you should avoid it. If your institution's mission is centred on digital and born-digital content, there is nothing to preclude you from showcasing this in your mission statement.

The World Digital Library (WDL) is a perfect example of a programme whose mission is driven entirely by collecting and aggregating digital content. While the word 'digital' isn't used in reference to its content, beyond the name of the programme itself, it is implicitly written into the mission statement through reference to the content's availability on the internet, and through their reference to the 'digital divide', as you can see in the following (WDL, n.d).

> The WDL makes available on the Internet, free of charge and in multilingual format, significant primary materials from all countries and cultures.

The principal objectives of the WDL are to:

- Promote international and intercultural understanding;
- Expand the volume and variety of cultural content on the internet;
- Provide resources for educators, scholars, and general audiences;
- Build capacity in partner institutions to narrow the digital divide within and between countries.

The NASA Space Science Data Coordinated Archive (Williams and Bell, 2016) references both analogue and digital content in its mission statement and operates very similarly to collection policies in that it more clearly defines the type of resources it collects:

> The NASA Space Science Data Coordinated Archive (NSSDCA) provides multidiscipline archive services, including an analog and digital archive from

> past NASA space science missions along with directories, catalogs, and access to widely distributed science data resources. The NSSDCA is responsible for the long term archiving and preservation of all space science data. The NSSDCA works closely in federation with the other Science Mission Directorate (SMD) sponsored discipline data archives. This federation is responsible for providing a coherent and coordinated space science data environment to improve quality, accessibility, and usability of NASA's space science data holdings for scientists, educators, and the general public.

Collection policies

Where you will most likely have to make the greatest adjustments is in your institution's collecting and appraisal policies. It is here where you will find the most detailed guidelines for allowable content and format. Having clearly defined policies and procedures in place before born-digital content is brought into your institution can ensure that only the material that fits the mission of the institution is acquired, stored and maintained.

Many existing collection policies address only the content of the potentially collected material and as such encompass all formats in which such content may be fixed. Other collection policies cite digital content broadly as an accepted format, and very few directly mention born-digital content as an accepted format. Some institutions do not yet have the facilities to manage digital or born-digital content and indicate this in their collection policies. Other institutions are able to manage only a particular set of digital file formats, which they often list and describe in their collection policies.

We will review a few example policies created for these various purposes so that you can craft your own policies based on the scenarios that best fit your own. As many well-defined collection policies are lengthy and detailed, we will review excerpts of relevant passages found within the longer policies.

Content-driven policy statements

Many institutions make it clear in their policies that they collect all material that has content that fits their mission, regardless of format. These content-driven policies allow for the inclusion of born-digital content, as long as this content fits the mission. A good example of this type of collecting policy statement is from the Massachusetts Institute of Technology (MIT) Institute Archives Records Collection Policy (1976).

> All records generated or received by the various administrative and academic offices of the Institute in the conduct of their business, regardless of the form in which they are created and maintained, are the property of the Institute and constitute archival material. The records covered by this policy include official printed material, correspondence, machine-readable files, record books, minutes, committee files, financial records, and associated paper.

Policies that include digital

There are some collection policies that directly specify which types of formats they will collect, and many of these cite digital or 'electronic' formats. For example, under 'type of materials and formats' in the University of Victoria Libraries' collections policy (n.d.), 'electronic files' are listed.

> The UVic Publications Collection includes monographs, serials and pamphlets.
> The archival material includes textual records, photographs, videos, audio cassettes, posters, microforms, maps and electronic files.

Interestingly, the Connecticut State Library Archives' Collection Policy (1996) states that it collects a wide variety of digital content, but includes provisos for the Archives' ability to preserve and provide access to the transferred records.

> The State Archives shall acquire motion picture films, video cassettes, audio recordings, machine readable records and other records on non-traditional storage media only for those records within the above defined categories. The State Archives reserves the right to refuse records falling within the collection policy if it cannot reasonably assume that it will have the necessary resources, including staff, working equipment or proper storage facilities to address the records' special conservation and access requirements.
>
> For machine readable records, the State Archives cannot possess and maintain every possible piece of hardware and software utilized within state government and the private sector. Therefore, the State Archives reserves the right to require that agencies utilizing unique hardware and software provide the State Archives with paper copies of any records scheduled as permanent/archival or appraised to possess historic value when presented for disposition.

Similarly, the University of Alabama at Birmingham (UAB) Libraries Digital Collections policy (n.d.) contains guidance as to which digital formats they can support, and states that unsupported formats will be preserved as bitstreams in the form in which they were deposited.

> Works added to UAB Digital Collections should be submitted in appropriate formats as specified in guidelines determined by Digital Collections staff. We offer full support for formats that are publicly documented, widely adopted, may be rendered by multiple software packages or have lossless data compression. Fully supported file formats (e.g., .pdf) are those that the UAB libraries will make readable and retrievable for the foreseeable future, employing migration and archival techniques as necessary. Partially supported file formats are those for which Digital Collection staff will recognize, but cannot guarantee full support for the foreseeable future. Examples of partially supported file formats are proprietary formats (e.g., .doc). Unsupported file formats are those that the Digital Collection Staff can only support as bit streams. Works will be preserved in the form of original deposit. When migration or other preservation strategies are required, the content, structure, and functionality of the files will be maintained when possible. Ongoing support will be provided for as many file formats as possible with the institutional resources that are available. Efforts will be made to monitor file format changes that may warrant transformation or reassessment, migration and onsite backup.

Born-digital-specific policies

While these are still rare, there are a few existing collection policies that explicitly include language to address born-digital content. The Irish Architectural Archive's acquisitions policy (2016) goes so far as to acknowledge that the majority of its content is born-digital.

> Given the ubiquitous use of information technologies in architectural practice and building recording, the vast majority of modern architectural records are 'born digital'. The Archive will accession digital material, and will, as part of the acquisition process, seek to acquire the metadata necessary to allow digital acquisitions to be preserved, accessed, migrated and used in an archival context over time. Required metadata will conform to the Dublin Core metadata standard or such other standard as the Archive may from time to time deem suitable. When material is acquired in digital

> format, the Archive may also seek hard copies, on and in stable media, of at least the principal drawings – main plans, sections and elevations – for all or for selected projects in the collection.

The Carolina Digital Repository's collection development policy (2018) includes an entire section devoted to born-digital content, a portion of which is included here.

> Born-digital bodies of work or portions of digital personal archives are materials created by a person or group of people to document their activities, such as creative works, activities within a business or research conducted. Materials in this category are like other acquisitions made by various collections units at UNC at Chapel Hill, differing primarily in their digital rather than analog nature. Examples may include but are not limited to: email correspondence, digital literary manuscripts, and research data.

Policies with digital content excluded

There are, of course, some institutions that do **not** want to collect digital, and subsequently born-digital, content. In some cases, it might not fit with the overall mission of the institution, or the institution may just not be ready to collect and preserve digitised or born-digital content. We can assume that since you are reading this book, this is not the case for you. Of course after reading this book you may decide otherwise – but we certainly hope not!

The University of Leicester Library's collection policy (2016) states that it does 'not *yet* [emphasis added] accept digital records for permanent preservation', though it does provide access to digitised content. The collection policy reads as follows.

> The majority of the archive collections comprise paper records. A significant proportion of the earlier acquisitions comprise artificial or antiquarian collections rather than true fonds originating from a specific organisation or individual in the course of their activities. The single biggest collection or fonds is that of the local newspaper, the Leicester Mercury, and comprises extensive series of photographic prints, negatives and newspaper cuttings. There is a very small proportion of parchment and audio-visual material and few maps and /or plans. The service does not yet accept digital records for permanent preservation and access as part of its archival holdings although it

does deliver content in the form of digital surrogates via a digital asset management system (CONTENTdm).

Gift agreements

Gift agreements are most commonly used in an archival environment where original content is donated to the institution. In many cases, born-digital content has come into libraries and archives in boxes among other material. Often, these boxes are simply shifted into the collection without much further ado. We have heard of times when boxes of disks and even whole computers were accessioned into an archival collection, and stored for several years. Only much later did the archivists discover that there was nothing of value on the computers, which they could have otherwise not acquired.

It is best to avoid this scenario by establishing a method to review and appraise the content of the digital media before bringing it into the collection. The simplest method of doing this is to ask the donor for a basic inventory of what is contained on the media. Where this is not possible, use the technology available to you to safely access and review the content on the media before accessioning it. We will cover how to do this work in Chapter 3. In cases where there may be hundreds of digital disks or where you may not have the technology readily available to access the content on the digital media, you can conditionally accept the media, but include the stipulation that the content may be returned, donated elsewhere or disposed of if it does not fit the collecting mission or appraisal policies. It is wise to include such stipulations in donor agreements, as is demonstrated in the University of Colorado Boulder Special Collections, Archives and Preservation Gift Agreement example that follows.

CU Boulder Special Collections, Archives & Preservation Gift Agreement

Thank you for your donation. Donations of published items, photographs, artwork, and archival materials are accepted by the Regents of the University of Colorado, on behalf of the University of Colorado Boulder, University Libraries, ('University') with the understanding that they will be considered for addition to the collection in accordance with University collection development policies. The University may return, appropriately dispose of or deaccession materials deemed unsuitable to the collection unless otherwise stipulated.

The University cannot by law provide appraisals for tax purposes. The responsibility of appraising donations remains with the donor.

Description of materials (i.e. books, papers):

Number of containers or items:

Additional information: Please list any additional requests or information regarding donated materials.

☐ Check here if you would like unaccessioned items returned to you.

Assignment of Rights: I irrevocably assign and convey the legal title, copyrights, and literary rights in as far as I hold them to the Regents of the University of Colorado, on behalf of the University of Colorado at Boulder, University Libraries. The University does not assume responsibility for infringement of copy or publication rights of manuscripts or photographs that are held by the creator or any other heirs, donors, or executors.
University Use of Donated Materials: The Donor grants the University the right to archive, display, reformat, digitise, and provide public access to his/her/their gift.

Digital Addendum
Deed of Gift Addendum for Collections with Electronic Records
The CU Boulder Libraries Special Collections and Archives Department acquires electronic records with the objective of making them available to researchers. In order to preserve electronic data and provide long-term access, the library will have to migrate or transfer material provided by the donor to new forms of media or file formats.

Actions specific to electronic records
The donor agrees that the following actions can be taken by the CU Boulder Libraries in order to provide access to the donated material:
- The donor grants permission to the library to make preservation and access copies of the materials for public use.
- The donor will disable passwords or encryption systems, if any, to allow access to the donated materials.
- The donor allows the library to recover deleted files or file fragments and provide access to the files.
- The donor allows the library to provide access to data that documents your use of computers or systems such as log files, system files and other data.

Personally Identifiable Information (PII)
The library will review material for any personally identifiable information and/or private information. Please let us know to the best of your knowledge if the electronic records contain any of the following:
__Social Security numbers
__Passwords or PINs
__Credit card numbers
__Financial records
__Medical records
__Licensed or pirated software
__Other records that have privacy concerns, please explain below:

Disposition of original transfer media
If the original transfer media and/or hardware are no longer needed by the library the donor has the option to have it returned, otherwise the library will securely dispose of it. Please let us know your preference: ____ Yes, please return ____ No, do not return

Stanford University's approach to selection in web archiving

Stanford University drew up comprehensive collection development guidance for web archiving. We share this use case with permission from Nick Taylor, who at the time of its writing was the Product and Service Manager for Web Archiving at Stanford. This guidance is a good example of how you might approach developing similar collecting strategies.

Our collection development guidance is intended to fulfill the following objectives:

- complement discipline-specific collection development policies;
- help curators decide what and, more importantly, what *not* to collect; and
- ensure that comparatively limited web archiving resources are deployed only for the most valuable content.

Focus on at-risk content
All web content is in some sense at-risk; this is, in fact, the raison d'être for web archiving. Particular categories of web content are more at-risk,

however, because they are of time-limited interest or purpose, subject to government censorship, disseminated by immature organizations, or for other reasons. Spontaneous events, including disasters, revolutions and trending social topics may briefly occupy the public spotlight, then fade from view. This unique and ephemeral content is especially deserving of our attention.

Complement existing collecting strengths

We have collecting strengths in particular areas, reflected by the research we support, our staffing for different subjects, our Special Collections, our relationships with donors and alumni, our geography and our institutional history. We provide added value when we consider web archiving as a potential component of a broader collecting plan and create web archives to complement other extant and prospective collections.

Observe resource constraints

A format-agnostic collection development policy will more than likely designate a broader range of web content as in scope for collecting than is practically feasible, given available web archiving resources. We should be mindful of collection dimensions that are most likely to increase costs. This includes not just the number of nominated websites but also their complexity (i.e. demanding additional staff time for crawl configuration and quality assurance) and contents (i.e. large files like video balloon storage requirements).

Consider what others are collecting

We are a member of an international community whose collective goal is collecting, preserving, and providing access to the historical web. Considering the cumulative and growing volume of information that has ever existed on the Web, even our aggregated efforts represent but a small fraction. We should therefore strive to identify existing web archives that overlap with areas where we intend to archive the Web ourselves and minimise duplication of effort. An enhancement to this approach is finding ways to provide seamless access to those external resources to our users, such as through topic guides, SearchWorks, or Memento.

Web archive holdings are not documented systematically, in terms of subject area, temporal coverage, language, top-level domain, or other identifiers, though research is underway that should simplify this. In the meantime, places to consult to discover existing web archives include: Archive-It's collections portal, the International Internet Preservation Consortium's list of member archives, the Wikipedia List of Web archiving initiatives, the Internet Archive Wayback Machine, and the UK Web Archive Memento aggregator service. Curators may often learn about and/or contribute to planned web archives through their discipline-specific communities of practice. If overlap with another web archive is discovered, we should additionally consider the depth and frequency of their archiving to determine whether it is still worthwhile for us to archive it.

Consider the access conditions of what others are collecting
National libraries, in particular, create web archives under legal frameworks that only permit limited access (e.g., on-premise, for designated research, etc.). While generally we should avoid duplicatively archiving web content that has already been preserved by another organization, the prospect of their not making it accessible should count in favor of our archiving it, as well.

Assess value to researchers
A fundamental challenge for selecting content is that its potential utility increases over time, as the risk of change to or loss of the original content increases and the archive takes on historical context. Through their relationship with faculty and awareness of the web resources that have been vital to research within a given subject area, curators are best positioned to identify the content that matters for future research.

Enable specific research use cases
The hope is that the rest of these guidelines yield web archive collections that are ultimately useful to researchers, broadly construed. Given that goal, specific researcher use cases that happen to contravene some of the guidance are still worth considering. For example, we were approached by researchers in the Political Science department with a scholarly use case for archiving 2014 congressional campaign websites. Strictly following the guideline to not duplicate other organizations' collecting efforts, it wouldn't have made sense to support the project, since the Library of Congress builds comprehensive election web archives every cycle. However, we also determined that the Library of Congress data could not be made available to the researchers in the time frame they needed it, so we worked out another way to enable the archiving in partnership with Archive-It.

Consider the appropriate archiving service
Even having concluded that some web content is worth saving, web

archiving isn't necessarily the most appropriate mechanism for capturing, storing, and re-presenting it. Web archiving is best suited to either where the 'object' of interest is a website, consisting of an arbitrary number of files that must be stored and re-presented in their original relationship to each other, or where it is important to preserve the temporal context of the web content, such that it could theoretically be later addressed temporally using Memento. The technical limitations of web archiving may also point toward alternative approaches.

Everyday Electronic Materials (EEMs) was built partly with web-accessible documents in mind. It is a better solution for that use case since the documents are discrete and preserving their temporal context is unimportant. Web-based video can be difficult to capture using crawler-based tools and demands outsized amounts of storage, relative to other web objects. The Stanford Media Preservation Lab is improving their support for digital video formats.

Prefer archiving content over links to content

Historical web addresses are valuable primarily, though not exclusively, for facilitating access to historical web resources. The web address is the key to discovering the range of temporal snapshots for a particular resource within Wayback; it can facilitate discovery of resources stored in other web archives; and it incidentally tells us about the content beyond the edges of what was captured.

On the other hand, accessing the historical web resources themselves presupposes that they have been archived. If there is value in capturing an aggregation of links on a particular topic, it is likely on account of the value of the websites that those links point to, so they should be considered for collection themselves. Depending on their origin, externally-curated lists of links can be a useful selection tool. For example, the Library of Congress uses the effectively crowd-sourced Wikipedia list of U.S. think tanks to seed their Public Policy Topics collection.

Prefer current and esoteric content

Current content is less likely to be represented in existing web archives than content that has been on the Web for a while. It matters also how content is linked to; on average, search engine results and shortened links are less prevalent in web archives than are resources that many stable websites link to. We should prefer content that is contemporary and/or not likely to be extensively linked to.

Conclusion

The selection of the born-digital content that your institution will acquire is tremendously important. There are thousands of different types of content that you will have the opportunity to select. You may have to face technological constraints which limit your ability to acquire valuable content, or you may decide to limit your institution's collecting only by its content-driven mission. Whatever the case, don't feel daunted. While this is important work, there is a lot of guidance out there to support you. We'll leave you with this quote from Sarah Barsness, in conversation with Bethany Anderson (2016) on the Society of American Archivists' blog, *Assigning Value*.

> There are just so many unknowns when it comes to digital material and how (or even if) it can be saved for decades to come. Don't let that uncertainty keep you from acquiring amazing collections that happen to be digital, because we'll never be able to preserve the things we don't try to save.

After reading this chapter, you should now have a better sense of:

- Types of born-digital content you could acquire at your institution
- General things to keep in mind when making collecting decisions
- What type of mission statement, collection policy, and donor agreements you will need to aid your collecting activities.

Further reading

Anderson, B. and Barsness, S. (2016) Acquiring and Appraising Born-Digital Material at the Minnesota Historical Society, in *Assigning Value: a blog by the Acquisitions and Appraisal Section of the Society of American Archivists*, https://appraisalsaa.wordpress.com/2016/07/27/acquiring-and-appraising-born-digital-material-at-the-minnesota-historical-society/.

A great interview between Bethany Anderson and Sarah Barsness about how the Minnesota Historical Society makes selection decisions for born-digital content.

Redwine, G., Barnard, M., Donovan, K., Farr, E., Forstrom, M., Hansen, W., Leighton John, J., Kuhl, N., Shaw, S. and Thomas, S. (2013) *Born Digital: guidance for donors, dealers, and archival repositories*, Council on Library and Information Resources,

www.clir.org/wp-content/uploads/sites/6/pub159.pdf.
Clear and relevant guidance on the whole acquisition process for born-digital content.

UNESCO/PERSIST Content Task Force (2016) *The UNESCO/PERSIST Guidelines for the Selection of Digital Heritage for Long-term Preservation*, International Federation of Library Associations.
A concise, international report providing guidance for cultural heritage institutions selecting digital content. English, French, Arabic, Lithuanian and Dutch versions available.

Reference

Hulme, T. E. (1911) A Note on the Art of Political Conversation, *The Commentator*, February 22, 1911.

CHAPTER 3

Acquisition, accessioning and ingest

> There are libraries, archives and collections out there with floppies. They probably never got funding or time to take the data off – there's a great chance the floppies are considered plain old acquisition items and objects, like books or a brooch or a duvet cover. They're not.
>
> (Jason Scott, *ASCII blog*, 2011)

Now that we have discussed major appraising and collecting concerns, let's get into the specific work of acquiring, accessioning and ingesting born-digital content into an archives or library collection. Before we do so, bear with us as we define these terms and cover the high-level principles that guide born-digital acquisitions. For our purposes here, **acquisition** refers to the physical retrieval of digital content. This could describe acquiring files from a floppy drive, selecting files from a donor's hard drive or receiving files as an e-mail attachment from a donor. In all cases, you now have physical control of the content. **Accessioning** refers to integrating the content into your archives or collections: assigning an identifier to the accession, associating the accession with a collection and adding this administrative information into your inventory or collection management system. **Ingest** is the process of placing your content into whatever repository system you have for digital content. This could be any solution from a simple but consistent file and folder structure to a full stack of storage and content management software. While each of these processes can sometimes be done in a single step, we will cover each in turn, and by the end of the chapter you should have a comprehensive overview of the initial steps in any born-digital workflow.

Principles of acquisition

The principles of acquisition of born-digital content flow from the general guidelines for acquiring all archival material. Yes, that's right: *respect des fonds* is still the guiding light for handling born-digital content. The principle, issuing from Natalis de Wailly at the Royal Archives of France in 1841, advises the grouping of collections by the body (roughly, the 'fonds') under which they were created and purposed. The two natural objectives flowing from *respect des fonds* are the retention of both provenance and original order. These objectives really get to the heart of our concerns in acquiring born-digital content – we want to avoid tampering with original order or losing sight of provenance each step of the way.

It can be surprisingly tricky to do this, and there have arisen a multitude of tools and techniques in the digital space to facilitate best practices. The whole field of digital forensics, as it has been adopted by the archives and cultural heritage communities, is designed to maintain original order and provenance. In general, the tools and techniques to do this come from the law enforcement and criminal investigation fields' overriding injunction to never alter evidence. Digital forensics comes into play for some types of born-digital acquisition, but by no means all, so we will cover other relevant acquisition techniques too.

Acquisition of born-digital material on a physical carrier

Forensics as practised by libraries and archives is most often centred on the acquisition of digital content from physical digital media items – floppy disks, data tapes, spinning-disk hard drives, USB drives (and other solid-state drives) and optical media. The number of collections containing this material is growing. To take a recent example, the University of Melbourne began working with the floppy disks and computers of the Australian writer Germaine Greer. This media contains voluminous amounts of her work and life, much unpublished and unseen, including floppy disks containing an unpublished book and two Mac computers – along with a hefty born-digital love letter to a fellow writer. That is a significant store of information located on digital media.

Getting material off these types of devices presents us with a few concerns. By virtue of the file system technology residing on these media, we have in our hands not just the donor's content, but also the context and environment of that content – the material's *original order* as it came to the library or archives, along with traces of the user's activity, potential remnants of past data, and system files and features not revealed to the regular user. All of this information can also constitute aspects of *provenance* as well, giving us information on the origin and ownership of the material. Therefore, simple copying of data from these devices is equivalent to disregarding this contextual information. This is the first cause for forensic technology in libraries and archives. Our second concern is that the mere *attaching* of this media to a computer, whereby that computer recognises the media attached to it, typically initiates a series of unprompted adjustments to the media by the computer. We will cover these adjustments shortly, but our takeaway here is that the simple connecting of a media item to a computer for copying can constitute the *destruction* of the contextual information as well, not just the benign disregard of it. This is the second cause for forensics in the field.

The file system

Because nearly all the contextual data that an archivist would be interested in is present in the file system of a media item, we will take a moment to describe the role of the file system. The file system is the main organizing system that an operating system uses to arrange the files and folders, both physically and through name assignment, on a disk. Similarly to a physical filing system, which provides organization for paper files, records and forms, a digital file system is a prescribed way for an operating system to organize the data on a computer. It keeps track of where data is on a disk, along with all the names you give to your files and folders. Along with these basic organizing tasks, the file system usually provides ways for the operating system to record dates and times associated with the files, such as the last time a file was modified, when it was created, the last time a file was opened and, in some cases, when the file was removed.

A file system is a piece of software that is subject to additions, refinements, reworking and other innovations, so any given file system will have different capabilities from another file system. Prominent file systems are and have been:

- the **FAT** file systems, in use in most older MS-DOS and Windows machines, and frequently used as a common *lingua franca* for portable drives – nearly every operating system understands FAT! We discussed FAT in the first chapter to give you an idea of how information can be organized on magnetic media.
- the **New Technology File System (NTFS)**, a successor file system to FAT developed by Microsoft and present in most Windows versions post-Windows NT (1993).

- the **Hierarchical File System (HFS)**, used in early Apple machines and media, its successor **HFS+** and **HFSX**, in use in all modern Apple systems, and the **Apple File System (APFS)**, a very recent successor (2017) to run across Apple's iOS and macOS machines.
- the **first, second, third and fourth extended file systems (ext1, ext2, ext3, ext4)** commonly run in Linux distributions.

You will probably run across one or more of these file systems in your own work, and may learn more about them as you require. For now, just demystifying all those initialisms should be enough!

Write blocking

Now that you have a sense of the important contextual data that the file system has knocking around on a piece of media, let's cover how that data can be tampered with if write blocking is not used; i.e. what can a computer write to an attached piece of media? We can't give a definitive list because these processes run in the background, unprompted by the user, and are subject to change based on the host computer's operating system and program updates. Nevertheless, here are a few examples of the tasks that software on a host computer may do upon detecting attached media.

- An operating system may read data from the files on the media, adjusting the access times to these files. It may do this to scan for viruses or to create a searchable index of the attached media's content for your convenience.
- An operating system may create temporary or hidden system folders and files on the attached device in order to help it manage the media.
- If the file system on both the host computer and the attached media is a *journaling system* – a file system that writes down what it is going to do before it does it – the host machine may scan for incomplete journal entries and complete or remove those entries for the attached media, again adjusting the received state of the device.

This is a short list, but we ultimately don't know, nor can we remain always knowledgeable, about what our work machines may do with the media we attach to them. Operating systems, the software on them and file systems themselves are changed and updated over time. For example, an antivirus suite may make adjustments to an attached media device. This is all the more reason to use write blocking whenever we reasonably can.

So, what is write blocking? Write blocking is the process of blocking all write commands to any partition or device. Older floppy disk media actually have this functionality built into the floppy disks themselves, in the form of either an adjustable read and write tab in 3.5" disks or a physical notch in 5.25" and 8" floppy disks (see Figures 3.1, 3.2 and 3.3 below and on the next page). Floppy disk drives will observe for these physical attributes and block writes appropriately. If you encounter CD-Rs or CD-ROMs in your collection, these newer media will also be write blocked as well.

However, much media remains open to writes, including hard drives, USB and other solid-state drives and tape media. The primary way to avoid writes to this type of media is the use of a *write blocker*, also termed a *forensic bridge*. These devices sit in between the target media (the media you are attempting to acquire data from) and the host machine (the computer you are using to acquire this data). They detect any write commands issuing from the host machine and either directly block these write commands, or bank the write commands in their own store while

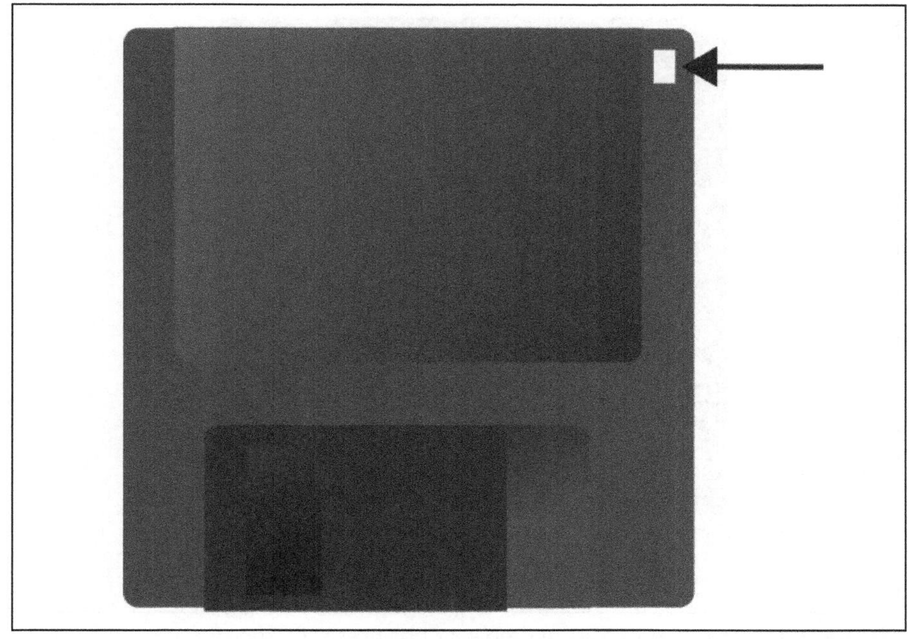

Figure 3.1 *If the 3.5" write tab is covered, the disk is* write-enabled

Figure 3.2 *If the 5.25″ notch is covered, the disk is* write-protected

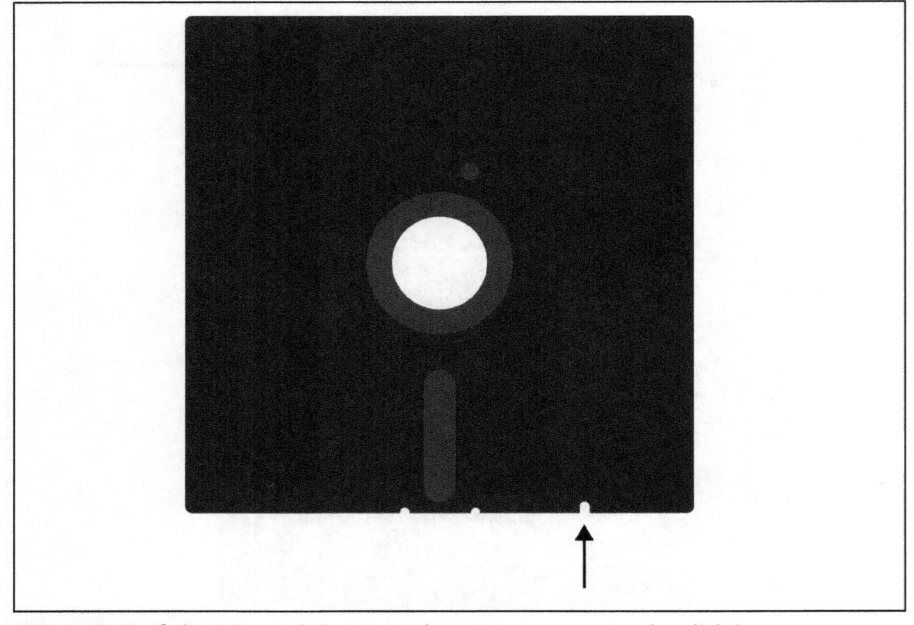

Figure 3.3 *If the 8″ notch is covered – or not present – the disk is* write-enabled

preventing the commands from applying to the target media. While it is a subtle adjustment in strategy, in either case writes from the host machine are blocked from the device. Write blockers can provide other useful features, such as detection of hidden partitions, block counts and a tally of bad sectors. Perhaps foremost among the extra functionality is the simple ability to *connect* a hard drive to the host machine, as write blockers come with an array of ports designed to attach to both the host machine and the target media. Write blocking and facilitating a physical connection to your host machine make these devices a critical piece of your acquisition workflow if you are encountering any number of writable media.

Write blocking devices can be replaced with a software write blocker as well. This software is run on the host machine and attempts to intercept and block write commands issuing from the operating system or other software. In some cases, this may be your only option, due to either budget constraints or unique physical circumstances. Nevertheless, software write blockers should be considered a secondary and less desirable solution to the problem. This is because such software is less reliable than write blocking devices, as it must *anticipate and detect* all processes on the host machine, as well as any other software, that may attempt a write on the target media. By contrast, a write blocking device need only *react* to any write commands issued, regardless of origin, and block those commands. The software write blocker's task is more difficult, as operating systems are not always fully documented or open source, nor are they static systems. Along with that, a user could install any number of programs, such as virus detection software, of which the software write blocker may not be properly aware.

Whether you are encountering media that is already write-only or media that remains writable, it is important to take the best steps you can to ensure write protection: check the tabs and notches on your floppy disks, verify that your CDs are in fact CD-Rs or CD-ROMs (although burning data to optical media is usually a multistep process and is less likely to occur without your knowledge) and use write blocking devices for other media – or if you must, a software write blocker instead. Taking this precaution will give you the best chance of preserving *all the information* on that media for future use!

The right drive for the right media

The second aspect of correctly attaching your target media to the host machine is to have the right equipment in place. It goes without saying that if you have a 5.25" floppy disk in hand, but no 5.25" drive, you will have an extraordinarily difficult time accessing data from that disk! In some cases, such as CDs and DVDs, acquiring a disc reader will not be too much of an imposition on either your budget or your time, as such readers are still commonly available from vendors and relatively inexpensive. As we move back further into computing's early years, locating and purchasing older drives becomes a little more cumbersome – but by no means out of reach. In the case of floppy disks, you will need to search for used drives. At the time of writing, eBay is still a good resource for locating these drives, and they are still within most budgets. 5.25" drives may cost as little as US$100 (c.£81.00), and 8" drives are often not too much more. If you can find a seller who indicates that the drive has been tested and calibrated, so much the better. There are also vintage drive vendors to be found online.

In the case of 3.5" drives, the market still has many USB-connected 3.5" drives. This may be appropriate if the 3.5" floppies are of the more modern, IBM-PC formatted variety, but you should be aware that floppy disks featuring older formats, such as Apple DOS, cannot be read by the USB-connected drives. These drives are only able to read IBM-PC formatted floppy disks. For this reason, you will probably want to acquire an actual vintage 3.5" drive, which can be used with a floppy disk controller to read a range of floppy disks. We will cover floppy disk controllers in the next section.

There are many media formats, from high-capacity (for their time, of course) Zip disks to mini optical discs and numerous data tape cartridges with countless others spanning both the USA and European industries, and many others across the world. It is beyond the scope of this book to cover every possible media format and the drives available to read from them, but be aware that there are many resources online to get started in this area. Both vintage computer enthusiasts and practitioners in the information science field will be of great help here.

Floppy disk controllers

Computers that were released with floppy disk drives, or that did not ship with drives themselves but were simply released during the era of floppy disks, all contained floppy disk controllers – a chip board with the circuitry to read and write from a floppy. Modern machines, of course, do not ship with floppy disk controllers. You may anticipate, then, a significant problem after acquiring your vintage floppy disk drive, as you will have no way to connect it to the host machine – and even if you did, the host machine may not be able to operate the attached floppy disk drive.

For vintage computing enthusiasts, for practitioners in the archives and library field or for individuals who simply want to rescue their personal data off old floppies, there has emerged a small market for modern floppy disk controllers – chip boards designed to connect to a modern machine via USB and facilitate a connection to an old floppy disk drive. Two prominent entries in this field are the FC5025 by Device Side Data and the KryoFlux, put together by the Software Preservation Society. The former is strictly for connection with 5.25" drives, while the latter can operate 5.25", 3.5" and even 8" drives (8" drives do require additional equipment, however). Again, it is beyond the scope of our overview here to delve into the use cases and specific procedures for these floppy disk controllers, but suffice to say that you will want to acquire these devices after you have secured your floppy disk drives. The particular board depends on the drives and disks you need to process, though the KryoFlux is the most flexible single device in this space. An added benefit is that these floppy disk controllers will also serve as write blocking devices – it never hurts to be extra cautious!

A breather!

We have covered a lot and we have not yet reached the point where we are actually copying data from the target media! So, before we touch on that last step, here is a review of what we have established so far.

1 In born-digital acquisition *respect des fonds* is still in play, so we want to capture original order, provenance and other contextual information.
2 Merely attaching target media to a host machine can alter the target media and remove the desired contextual data.
3 In addition, simply copying the files off the target media will not capture these important pieces of information.
4 Because of 2, we want to practise *write blocking* with our target media.
5 Because of 3, we want to take *full disk images* of the target media instead of the more common operation of file copying.

Hopefully, summaries 1–4 make sense now. To close out our section on born-digital materials on physical carriers, let's talk about disk images.

Disk images and the file system

A disk image is a single capture of the entire content and structure of a data storage device. It is a bit-level identical copy of a piece of media. When you copy a file or files from a location, the operating system looks for the various parts and pieces of the file, corrals them together and produces a new copy of that file at whatever destination you specified. (You may recall that we described this basic process in Chapter 1 when talking about the FAT file system.) By contrast, when you create a disk image, the software program moves through the target media sector by sector, copying each in the sequence in which it appears, and wrapping up the whole output in single logical file. (The file may be broken into component files if you are imaging a large target media, such as a multi-gigabyte hard drive. This is done simply to make the file easier to transfer, but it is still one logical file.)

A disk image allows the preservation of all contextual data – how a file is organized on a volume, the volumes themselves, the directory structure, any partial or deleted-but-extant data and all file system metadata. How is this done? Again, imaging approaches the target media as a linear sequence of sectors – blocks of data – and copies those one by one. Imaging doesn't look at files *per se*. Instead, by operating at a level below the level of files, the process has the opportunity to capture *everything* – the content and the structure – present on the media.

In summary, here is a short list of the many aspects a disk image captures.

- Disk images capture both the contents and the structure of a data storage device, such as the volume and directory structure, some of which may not be apparent to a regular user.
- Disk images capture both allocated data (i.e. written and listed) and unallocated data (e.g. partial or whole data from overwrites, deletes or previous file versions).
- Disk images retain file system-level metadata, which may include creation and last modified times for files, among other timestamps and values.
- Disk images can retain all this information described in a single file,

or in a logical series of files, which may make it easier to manage and retain.
- Disk images can support the archive concepts of provenance and context of the data on the storage device through the features listed here.

There is a wide range of software – much of it free – to make images of various media. Disk images can be made of any media attached to a host machine: floppy disks, tapes, hard drives and solid-state drives, and optical discs. The format of the final file constituting the disk image is either 'raw' – the base sectors collected into a single output – or some other format that wraps around and in some way embellishes that raw stream. Some of the advantages of these disk image formats, such as EWF and the Advanced Forensics Format are the following:

> - The images can be stored as losslessly compressed or uncompressed files. ('Losslessly' indicates that the compression process does not remove data when the file is decompressed.)
> - The images can be split into multiple storage containers (useful especially for large hard drive images).
> - Metadata created during the imaging process can be packaged with the disk image itself.
> - The images can be parsed at the file system level without explicitly extracting the raw image.
>
> (BitCurator Consortium. n.d.)

For these reasons, you may consider using an image format beyond the raw stream. We recommend EWF at the time of writing, as the format features a great tool base in the *libewf* library, available on GitHub.

File extraction and examination

As noted in the previous section, disk images allow you to manage and transport all the files from a disk in a single file. At some point, it is likely that you will want to extract the files from the images for processing or for your users. There are typically two primary ways to perform this action. The first is to rely on the underlying functions of your operating system to access the disk image as a volume on the computer. In many cases, this is done by simply double-clicking the disk image file, or right-clicking the icon to display an option to open or mount the volume. 'Mount' is a Unix process to create a location of the disk image in your computer's directory tree. Regardless of the way you do this, you will be relying on the operating system's knowledge of the volume and the file system therein to mount the image and allow you to browse its contents as you would any other disk location.

The second method is to use software specifically designed to mount the volume and view or extract the contents. There is a range of software in this space; two great offerings are the BitCurator Disk Image Access Tool, available in the BitCurator environment, and HFSExplorer, designed specifically to mount HFS volumes. A processing suite like Archivematica deploys tools as well to extract files from disk images.

Hex editors

Sometimes, disk images do not mount. There are several reasons why a disk may not mount: an unfamiliar file system or volume format; bad sectors resulting from bad or incorrect reads; or the media may simply be damaged beyond the point where correct reads are possible without professional conservation work (if then). A full examination of possible solutions when you encounter a disk image is beyond our scope here, but we do want to introduce a type of software that can help you learn about what is on the disk image itself – even if you can't mount it. This software will be equally adept at peeking into files that you can render back with the software at hand, so it can be quite handy.

The software type is called a **hex editor**. We touched on hexadecimal notation in the first chapter where we saw that this notational system uses a base of 16 characters (0–9, then A–F) and can function as another encoding of data. Here we'll encounter hexadecimal again when we peek into the raw data of a file. Typically, however, you won't need to interpret hexadecimal, only understand how it plays into what the hex editor is showing you.

As you may expect, there are many hex editors on any operating system. The BitCurator suite comes with the GHex editor, and we have displayed in the following figures, the Hex Fiend editor available on macOS. The key function to understand about a hex editor is that it does not interpret the data of the disk image or file in any way, like a web browser interprets the source code of a web page to render it to you – a hex editor only displays data. Hex editors also allow you to directly edit the binary data of the file displayed, but that is not what we'll be doing. (In that sense, 'hex editor' is a bit of a misnomer for our purposes – 'hex viewer' is more accurate.)

In Figure 3.4, we are looking at a JPEG file. The highlighted data shows us the camera used to take the picture – a bit of metadata embedded in the file. We also have the date the image was taken, at least according to the time and date on the Canon PowerShot. In the left pane is the byte address of the file, from the first byte at the top to the last byte at the bottom. In the middle pane are the hexadecimal values for the bytes of the file, again in linear sequence, from the start at the top left to the very last byte (the whole file is not pictured here). Every pair of hexadecimal notation equals one byte, and if that data is renderable as ASCII plain text, you will be able to read that text in the right pane (data that doesn't correspond to an ASCII value is usually rendered as a '.'). This last component is the primary reason you would use a hex editor – to gain some insight into what data you have on hand. If we could not 'see' this JPEG because it had been corrupted beyond repair, here we would at least gather some metadata on it.

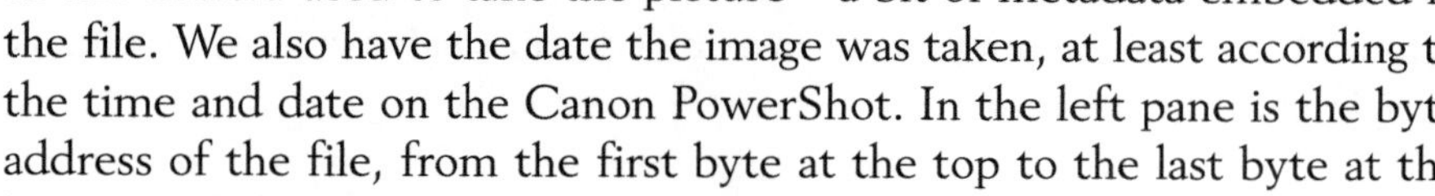

Figure 3.4 *Snippet of hex editor display of a JPEG image file*

In the screenshot in Figure 3.5, we are looking at a floppy disk image. We've highlighted again some plain text that we can read. We can pick out a few key pieces of information here – we seem to be reading instructions for a piece of software titled DGS, version 2.1, and it is a piece of software designed to run in the older DOS environment. From here, we can at least

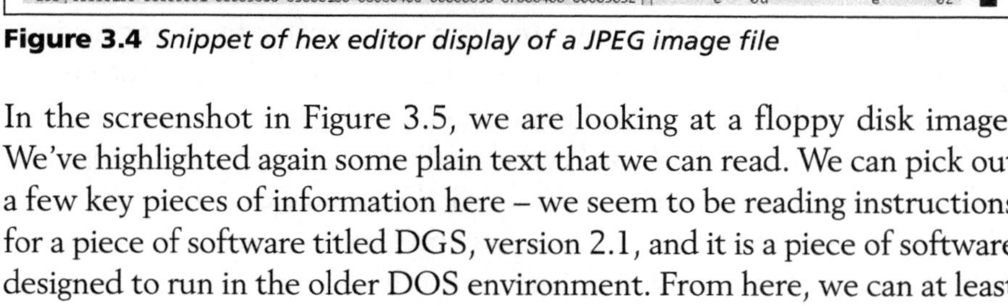

Figure 3.5 *Snippet of hex editor display of a disk image file*

begin to research what software this may be, with the assumption that that software is on the disk image – or at the very least, instructions for it – even if we cannot mount the disk image at the present time. These two examples demonstrate that if file extraction fails for a disk image, or if the disk image itself doesn't mount or otherwise can't be browsed, taking a look at the problematic data with a hex editor can give you some valuable insight into the contents.

Digital media disposition and identification

So, you have connected the digital media to your host computer, have forensically taken the contents off that device and can move to processing that content. What do you do with the physical media now? You can either choose to retain that item or securely dispose of it.

Why would you keep a media item when all the data has been copied from it? Like other 3D objects and ephemera that an archive or library retains, you may decide that the floppy disk, the USB stick or the external hard drive donated to you has value in the context of the collection. It may feature labelling from the creator, or other marks and traces that could be interest to researchers and users (as in Figure 3.6). You may decide that the digital media item is simply old enough and rare enough that you believe it is worthwhile to retain it for its novelty or exhibition value. Works and records produced on computers, distributed through computers and viewed on computers can often suffer from not having a physical association, so a media item that can provide that totemic or representative function is not insignificant.

One reason you should *not* keep a media item is as an extra copy. We will discuss storage preservation and digital repositories in Chapter 5, but the immediate point here is that your preservation strategy should be robust enough that you will not need to rely on scattered copies of the data found in floppies and CDs in your stacks and shelves. We understand the temptation to retain a media item as yet another backup 'just in case', but if this is the only reason you are keeping a box of USB sticks, we suggest that you instead responsibly recycle or destroy those items and let your preservation system take care of retention.

What are good reasons for deaccessioning digital media items? If the items contain no artefactual value, no significant traces of the original user or are only transporting devices for the data, it can be a good idea to return them to your donor or to recycle them. For example, you may receive

Figure 3.6 *Eight-inch floppy disk with significant labelling and creator marks* (Photo courtesy of Woody and Steina Vasulka)

several hard drives and CDs from a local politician's office at the end of their term. The office staff acquired the relevant e-mail inboxes, document folders, digital videos of the politician's speeches, along with numerous other records of the politician's work and loaded these all onto the external drives and CDs that you now have. Even if you decide to take forensic copies of the media to preserve any timestamps that could still be associated with the files, there's a strong argument that the physical items themselves carry no value for researchers – they are only the items used to carry the data from the politician's office to yours.

Assuming that you are keeping the media, you will want to assign an identifier to that media, and find some way to physically associate or attach that identifier to the item itself. A good identifier is going to depend upon your own naming conventions for your institution, and we recommend a straightforward policy where possible. For example, appending a sequential number to a collection name or collection accession number may be all that is needed:

```
bakerSmith042015-001
```

In the above example, the institution uses a lastnameFirstnameMMYYYY for the unique identifier of an accession, and we append a three digit sequential number to that to record a disk in that collection.

Once you have decided on a strategy for identification, you need to consider how you will associate that identifier with the item. Particularly if you are managing a collection with a large number of digital media items that you are electing to retain, having identifiers for each will be very important. Since digital media items come in so many shapes and sizes, we can't recommend a single best way to attach your identifiers to your media. However, let's keep a few points in mind:

- 5.25" and 8" disks, and to a lesser extent 3.5" disks, have sensitive platters underneath the plastic casing. You do not want to press hard on that casing, and you especially do not want to press hard with a fine writing point on the casing!
- Internal hard drives with metal chassis are more durable, by contrast, and a permanent marker may be sufficient here.
- Ensure that you are not obscuring any of the original markings or traces that moved you to retain the device in the first place.

We have found **artist tape** to be a good solution to applying identifiers for most media. Often used on paper and canvas, this type of tape is acid free and designed to be taken off the object without leaving residue. While it will surely lose its tackiness over time, replacing it should not be too great an imposition. Moreover, this strategy has the benefit of allowing you to not write directly on top of the media, and enabling you to remove the identifier for amendment or exhibit display. The exception to this strategy is optical media. If you cannot apply an identifier to the disc's case or sleeve – or do not want to – we recommend instead a felt-tip water-based marker, which you can use to write the identifier on the innermost circle of the disc, which does not contain any data.

Physical carrier wrap-up

While it has taken a little while to get there, you now have a complete overview of the critical pieces of acquisition for born-digital materials on a physical carrier: preserving context, write blocking and producing disk images. We will be touching on these aspects in later chapters as well, so do not despair if all of the aspects are not entirely lucid for you yet! Bear in mind as well that these are only brief overviews of each critical piece – as you build the workflows yourself you will become more and more familiar with the needed knowledge.

Before we leave here, it is important to reiterate that there are also cases where forensic copying of data from the target media is not needed. For instance, you may receive data from a donor on a portable hard drive, where the donor has already prepared copies for you – similar to the politician's office example described above. In these cases the media you have in your library or archives is not the original media used by the donor, but only a temporary storage device for transferring the data. In still other cases, you may determine that the contextual information is simply not germane or of research interest – perhaps the content on the drive really is the only information that needs to be preserved, or for which you have an agreement to preserve. Some state or national archives will fall into this category – the acquisition goal is narrowed just to the content of the records. While we believe it is better to err on the side of preserving more – with the understanding that some elements can be redacted as needed – there are cases where forensic tools and techniques are not the best solution.

Checksums and checksum algorithms

Before we discuss our next category of born-digital materials, let's take a moment to acquaint ourselves with **checksums** and **checksum algorithms**.

These sound like fairly technical concepts – and they are! But checksums and their utility to archives and libraries are actually fairly straightforward. Moreover, you will encounter references to checksums quite frequently in discussions of born-digital processing and preservation. We'll point out a few of the top applications of this technology as well.

Checksums are most commonly seen as alphanumeric values – for example, `5408dd96274b3373af6d5ef74ddd92da`. These values correspond to a specific file or block of data, and each alphanumeric value *uniquely* identifies that file or block of data. A checksum value is created through a checksum algorithm – a complex formula for deriving the alphanumeric value from the data you point it to.

When a checksum algorithm is run against a file, you get a unique value associated with that file – essentially a fingerprint of that file! That allows you to track that file across systems and ensure that no errors in its integrity have occurred, either in storage or in transmission from one place to another. Before we get into applications, however, let's look at an example.

Let's say I have a very simple text file with one sentence in it: 'The fox ate the floppy.' That's it. Now, I want to create a checksum for this file. (I spent a long time drafting this sentence, and I'd like to know it's safe.)

```
'The fox ate the floppy.' ->
5408dd96274b3373af6d5ef74ddd92da
```

There we are. Now, let's say I go back to this text file and make an adjustment. I want the fox to be even more gluttonous: 'The fox ate the floppies.' Let's run that same checksum algorithm again.

```
'The fox ate the floppies.' ->
a6223bbcd1243dfbca1c2c8f14b6c4f6
```

Notice here how the checksum, the unique value identifying the file with my selected checksum algorithm, is not only different – it is *very* different. Even a human can quickly scan these two alphanumeric values and see that the one is not anything like the other. We know that the author has adjusted something in that sentence.

Checksums are often used for just this reason, but at a scale no person could do (naturally). That is, a checksum algorithm is selected, it is run against tens, hundreds, thousands (or more) of files, and an entire index of checksums is created. We will call this Checksum List A. Later, stewards of the content rerun that same algorithm and the files, and compare this new group of checksums, Checksum List B, with List A. If there is a mismatch, we know the data has been adjusted in some way. That could be an undocumented change (perhaps an expected change, but no new checksum was generated to update List A), a storage error, or an error in transmission when the file was being moved. This can tip us off to problems we may have in our systems or practices. Do we not have a policy for a new checksum to be generated when we make edits? Is a hard drive failing? Do our network transfers need extra verification?

As you may expect, many processing softwares run checksums on the material processed, and many repository systems create checksums when material is taken in. Disk image container formats will create a header containing a checksum for the contained raw disk image as well. The applications are really innumerable, because having a fingerprint of a file allows handlers of that content – and those handlers may change a great deal over time – to be assured that the content in hand is accurate.

Finally, let's talk about those checksum algorithms. There are quite a few available, and they often sport lovely names like MD5, SHA1 and SHA2 (a family of functions containing SHA-224, SHA-256, SHA-384 and SHA-512). These algorithms feature different methodologies, and the later algorithms, such as the SHA2 family, provide better security from reverse engineering and more collision resistance – lowering the likelihood that two different files will create the same checksum. We most commonly encounter and use MD5, SHA1 and SHA256, and we think all of these are sufficient for the preservation task at hand. There are many known security holes for MD5 and even SHA1, but keep in mind that these are most often security gaps in the context of adversarial environments. Cultural heritage is typically not the target of information-cracking campaigns – but if you believe your organization may be the target of such attacks, you will want to consider higher security algorithms.

Acquisition of network-born materials

Thus far we have looked at born-digital materials coming to your library and archives on physical media – a professor's floppy disks, an office hard drive from a local politician or CDs containing photos and videos of an event. Of course, a great deal of material resides not on a physical carrier at hand, but is routinely accessed and found online. These materials include some of the most popular and frequently accessed formats, such as websites, social media content (Twitter posts, Facebook walls and Instagram photos) and e-mail. We are calling this type of material **network-born** – while this content can be downloaded to a machine, its real 'home' is online, on a network. Acquiring network-born material calls for a different set of guidelines.

Websites: in-browser save

One of the oldest and most immediate methods of preserving a web page is to use the browser's save function. This allows the browser to preserve a local copy of the web page in a number of formats, depending upon the browser: HTML, PDF or some other format that wraps the images, text and markup into a legible whole. While this method is expedient, it does come with significant limitations that generally make other capture options more attractive. The first limitation is that this method captures only a *page*, not a site. A site consists of one or more pages which you can view in your browser. For example, Amazon.com is a site which consists of an ever fluctuating and expanding number of pages featuring its products and services. Similarly, Wikipedia contains innumerable pages constituting its articles, while Wikipedia.com is the site itself. If you were to use the in-browser save function on either of these sites, you would save the page currently displayed, but not the entirety of the *site*.

Different web browsers can feature different page-saving formats, and this can be considered a second limitation. Along with HTML and PDF, some browsers also support the MIME Encapsulation of Aggregate HTML Documents (MHTML) format, also referred to as MHT due to the common *.mht* extension used for the saved file. MHTML is an open source format derived from the EML e-mail storage format, designed to wrap all page elements into a single file. Mozilla offers the Mozilla Archive Format (MAFF) in its Firefox browser, a format which it maintains as open source. Apple's Safari browser uses its own *.webarchive* format, which, similar to MHTML and MAFF, folds all the component parts of a single page into one file. Because of this range of formats, we recommend sticking with either a straightforward HTML save or a PDF save. The HTML save will have the disadvantage of saving multiple files and directories which constitute the whole of the web page, and these will need to be kept together. However, you can be assured that any browser will be able to load this page by pointing it to the main page file (it's usually titled *index.html*, or simply look for the top-level *.htm* or *.html* page wherever you chose to save the page on your computer). The PDF save will have the disadvantage of rendering the page as a non-interactive document which nevertheless preserves the look of the page. However, you will need to maintain only a single file in this case. Both of these options avoid the potential support and interoperability pitfalls of more ambitious formats.

Along with the actual acquisition you have made through this method, it would be prudent to document how you did so. A simple text file that dates the download and describes the browser and save format used is sufficient, and will provide future users with the provenance information that they may need to best evaluate the saved site.

Websites: the WARC format

Sites that have been crawled are commonly saved in the Web Archive Container or WARC format. The WARC format wraps all the crawled data from a site into a single container, with the metadata and indexes required to unpack that file and optionally to browse the content offline. Importantly, the WARC format is designed to capture a whole site – all the pages hosted in a single domain. This is a dramatically expanded function from the in-browser save, which can target only the page you are viewing. The WARC format is open and is described thoroughly in ISO 28500:2009; there has been growing software support for the format since its introduction.

WARC serves well as a preservation format because it records important aspects of provenance either in its header or in other record files: characteristics of the crawler used (hang tight, we will talk about crawlers in the next section!), all the requests from that crawler and the responses from the site's server, a record identifier and a timestamp. Here is an example of the metadata available in a WARC's header from the International Internet Preservation Consortium (IIPC) Framework Working Group's *Information and documentation – The WARC File Format* document.

```
WARC/0.16
WARC-Type: warcinfo
WARC-Date: 2006-09-19T17:20:14Z
WARC-Record-ID: <urn:uuid:d7ae5c10-e6b3-4d27-967d-
34780c58ba39>
```

```
Content-Type: application/warc-fields
Content-Length: 381
software: Heritrix 1.12.0 http://crawler.archive.org
hostname: crawling017.archive.org
ip: 207.241.227.234
isPartOf: testcrawl-20050708
description: testcrawl with WARC output
operator: IA_Admin
http-header-user-agent:
Mozilla/5.0 (compatible; heritrix/1.4.0
+http://crawler.archive.org)
format: WARC file version 1.0
conformsTo:
http://www.archive.org/documents/WarcFileFormat-
1.0.html
```

A WARC file can even record alternate and formatted versions of harvested files if the crawler has been specified to perform these types of migrations. You can read a full specification of the WARC format at the ISO page cited here, and you can even download examples of WARC files at the Internet Archive (https://archive.org/details/ExampleArcAndWarcFiles.). Tools also exist, such as the suite managed at the Archives Unleashed Project online, that can extract a WARC's provenance information, allowing you to conduct useful analyses of your captured site content. The WARC format is therefore far more than a copy of a website – it is an important record of acquisition. We recommend targeting this format for the long-term retention of your crawled sites whenever possible.

Web crawlers: HTTrack and wget

We noted above that the WARC format can describe the crawler used to capture a site. Web crawlers are software used to capture or 'harvest' content, metadata or both from a site. Crawlers have been used for a variety of purposes. One of the earliest and still common uses of a web crawler is to create a queryable index for search engines. A second use for a web crawler, of course, could be archiving – telling the crawler's software to browse a site with the intention of retaining the harvested data.

There are several web crawlers designed with this in mind, and we will briefly cover two of them here: one available with a graphical front end, and another just available through your computer's command line. There are a range of other web crawlers available to use, but we think these two are the most immediately useable, and will give you a good understanding of the decision process for crawling a site you want to capture.

HTTrack

HTTrack has the benefit of providing both a command line interface and a GUI. The graphic user interface comes in two flavours, as a Windows program and as a web front end. In either case, you will be presented with a field to input the site address you wish to capture, along with a range of parameters you can set to more finely control the crawl. These settings allow you to stagger your calls to the site so that the server(s) running the site do not shut out your requests for access, along with options to set the number of links to follow within the site, logging and index settings, and several more. Once a capture is complete, all files are downloaded into the folder specified by the user, mirroring the structure of the site itself.

HTTrack provides its own manual that can help you to discover which options are best for the capture you want, and we'll cover a few of these in the next section discussing `wget`. As mentioned above, there are other crawlers available, but as of this time of writing, HTTrack continues to be maintained, with a community surrounding the software.

wget

For users unfamiliar with the command line on their computer, `wget` will have a higher barrier to use. That being said, if you are able to access this interface on your computer and install the program, `wget` can be a very expedient way to capture a website with a single command. `Wget` is a general purpose browser and downloader of web content, developed originally in 1996 for Linux machines and subsequently ported to other popular platforms like Windows and macOS. In 2016, a new addition to the program allowed it to save the targeted site into the WARC format, greatly expanding its utility for the library and archives communities.

The basic syntax of the `wget` command is straightforward:

```
wget <URL>
```

The <URL> component is the address of the site you wish to archive. A number of options can be set in between the `wget` command and the site address, which can make your crawl better suited for long-term archiving. Foremost among these is the option to save the resulting data in the WARC format.

```
wget --warc-file=YOUR_FILENAME <URL>
```

In the above command, we have set an option to have `wget` save the file in the WARC format with whatever name you wish to specify for YOUR_FILENAME (for example, 'test-archive.warc').

There are numerous other options you can set with your `wget` command, which we recommend investigating. You can find useful guides on this subject online. Deciding on the options you would like to use with `wget` can take a little time initially, but once you have decided on those options, that set can be repeated for any site you wish to capture. To start you on your way, however, let's take a look at three options that we think should be included in every crawl.

1. `-mirror`: This option actually activates several other options which allow `wget` to capture the site recursively, in its entirety (stylesheets, images and so on).
2. `-convert-links`: This option adjusts the hyperlinks in your site capture to relative paths, so that you can browse the site offline (rather than having the captured site's links point to the online pages).
3. `-o <LOG_FILENAME>`: This option produces a log (saved as whatever you specify for `<LOG_FILENAME>`) of `wget`'s activities during the capture. We always want to record what we did whenever we can do so – for provenance!

You can capture a few test sites and experiment with these options and others referenced online.

On-demand capture: Wayback Machine, Archive-It, Webrecorder.io

Because of the complexity and high overhead involved with systematically archiving sites, there are services available to libraries and archives that allow you to simply use them online as you need them. This can be a great option if your institution doesn't have the appetite for bringing this technology in-house.

The Wayback Machine is an initiative of the Internet Archive, a US-based non-profit organization that has accrued a large collection of archived websites, among other materials. The Wayback Machine is a tool that can be used to browse older archived sites by typing the address into its search bar, or to prompt the archiving of a specific site by typing that address into its save bar. This sets the crawlers at the Internet Archive onto the site, and in due time that site will be aggregated into the whole of the Internet Archive. In this manner you can save a site or page on demand. The drawback here is that the saved content is not hosted at or affiliated to your institution, though you will of course be able to point to, link to and reference that content once it is processed into the Internet Archive.

As you might imagine, there is a market space for the Wayback Machine's function that *does* affiliate the content with the institution prompting the archiving. This service is called Archive-It, and it is a paid service offered by Internet Archive. The process is similar to the Wayback Machine, where the institution provides a URL (or a 'seed', as the terminology goes) to the Archive-It service, with various optional parameters, and the service then proceeds to capture. In this case the institution will have monitoring controls and a few methods to adjust the scope of the crawl. If your institution is able to allocate funds for archiving web content, this service may be an option.

A third option, Webrecorder.io, takes a different approach to archiving a site or page. Web crawlers do a good job of capturing 'static' content – fixed pages, documents, images and numerous other bits of a website. However, much of the modern web is not static – it is dynamic, with content often adjusted to the specific user on the site, and new content appearing only when the user scrolls or focuses on a certain element of the page. Think of the Amazon.com front page experience, which is highly tailored to the logged-in user, or simply the approximate geographic location of the user. Or consider the Facebook wall, which reveals new content only when the user scrolls down the page. While crawlers can capture some of this content, the more dynamic a site is designed to be, the more likely it is that a crawler will miss content you aim to capture, which in turn compels the user to run multiple crawls or adjust the crawl settings.

Webrecorder.io attempts to address this problem by allowing on-demand site capture that is bounded by what the user does on the site during a set session. In this approach, the user goes to a site, hits 'Record' and then browses the site in whatever manner allows capture of the content of interest. Upon completion, the user saves and the recording session concludes. At this point the user may download the recording session (again, it will download as a trusty WARC) and play this file back in a separate app, Webrecorder Player. The strength of this approach is that it allows a highly targeted, curated acquisition of content that better conveys the experience of browsing the site and the dynamism of the content. A natural drawback of this method is that it does ask the user to spend whatever time is required on the actual site to record that dynamic content.

Existing web archives

We mentioned earlier the Internet Archive, which runs both the Wayback Machine and Archive-It. While its collection of captured web content is expansive, it is not the only web archive operating, but is in fact one among numerous others. A great way to discover these other archives, and to learn more about internet-archiving initiatives worldwide, is to reference the IIPC member list and website. The IIPC (see Further Reading) was established in 2003 and has since seen organizations from over 45 countries join in a larger effort to preserve knowledge found on the internet.

Another excellent way to explore existing web archives is through the Time Travel search site. This service searches a growing aggregation of web archives for captured content from a single search point, and typically performs this function through the use of the Memento protocol (RFC 70989), a formal process for searching and recalling archived sites. Time Travel can even attempt reconstruction of a site from a certain past point in time through Memento's 'Reconstruct' function, which searches for shared components of the requested site which may be available in other captured sites, along with any approximate, older versions of the requested site.

Finally, we note existing web archives here because it may be advantageous to your library or archives to be aware if targeted content is already being managed by an archive. If this is the case it may not preclude your organization's desire to steward that content under its own charter, but it may affect the decision-making process.

E-mail

While we don't have numbers, it's fair to estimate that most modern correspondence occurs via e-mail. Once a ground-breaking technology preceding even the internet itself, e-mail is now a daily part of most individuals' lives. Correspondingly, it is a major collecting interest for many archives and libraries, at both the level of the individual (for example, the poet Robert Creeley e-mail archive at Stanford University) and the organization (the Enron E-mail Dataset resulting from the 2001 US federal investigation). While e-mail is not nearly as complex as most websites, as a piece of digital content it does have a couple characteristics that we need to keep in mind when acquiring it.

The first characteristic is the saved file format of the e-mail itself. As a bundle of data running over a network, routed through e-mail servers and being finally received by a mail client, e-mail has a highly codified structure, presently laid out in RFC 5322. This documentation specifies elements of the e-mail such as the header, the subject line, the from and to addresses, along with a host of other properties. An agreed-upon data structure is of course immensely valuable for a technology like e-mail, which needs to travel across multiple computer systems in a reliable and predictable fashion. Unfortunately, the same standardisation does not apply to the format in which an e-mail is *saved* on a computer by an e-mail client. In this arena, there are a number of more or less viable formats.

We think the most straightforward and easily managed format for single e-mails is the .eml format. This format is in use by many mail clients, and many of them can export or save the e-mails they manage to this format. Eml stores the content of the e-mail in a plain text encoding according to the widely accepted Multipurpose Internet Mail Extensions (MIME) standard. Attachments to an e-mail are also stored according to the MIME standard. Because of the wider use, open standard and plain encoding, .eml is an expedient and reasonably safe way of saving single e-mail files.

Regardless of the format you save into, the *completeness* of the e-mail is paramount. This means that all elements of the e-mail are saved. That includes the attachment, the from and to fields, any cc fields and so on. The header of the e-mail is typically hidden from the user because it contains a good deal of technical information not germane to simply reading the message itself. Here's an example of an e-mail header:

```
Received: from cy4pr02cu001.internal.outlook.com by
CO2PR03MB2152.namprd03.prod.outlook.com with HTTP
via
CY4PR02CA0019.NAMPRD02.PROD.OUTLOOK.COM; Wed, 20 Sep
2017 19:58:00 +0000
```

```
Received: from
CY1PR03MB2185.namprd03.prod.outlook.com
([10.166.206.146]) by
CY1PR03MB2185.namprd03.prod.outlook.com
([10.166.206.146]) with mapi id
15.20.0056.018; Wed, 20 Sep 2017 19:57:59 +0000
From: John J Smith <John.Smith@College.EDU>
To: Jane Smith <Jane.Smith@EmailPlace.COM>
Subject: Time off notice
Thread-Topic: Time off notice
Thread-Index: AdMySsGEO5PSgzNeQDmruGuEyP48jg==
Date: Wed, 20 Sep 2017 19:57:59 +0000
Message-ID:
<CY1PR03MB21851EA631D0CB0FF63424FDE4610@CY1PR03MB218
5.namprd03.prod.outlook.com>
Accept-Language: en-US
Content-Language: en-US
X-MS-Has-Attach:
X-MS-Exchange-Organization-SCL: -1
X-MS-TNEF-Correlator:
<CY1PR03MB21851EA631D0CB0FF63424FDE4610@CY1PR03MB218
5.namprd03.prod.outlook.com>
MIME-Version: 1.0
```

This is actually only the top portion of an e-mail header, but it conveys the vitality of this information, ensuring that you have not just e-mail aliases ('John J Smith') but the e-mail addresses themselves, times of transfer and routing information. In terms of verifying authenticity and completeness, the e-mail header information is essential, so ensure that the save format includes this element.

E-mails are often managed not individually but by group – it isn't uncommon to want to acquire an entire mailbox for preservation. That mailbox may be the user's inbox, the user's 'sent' mailbox, which contains all their outgoing missives, or some other mailbox. In these cases we need a different format than .eml, and here the best choice is .mbox. Unlike .eml, .mbox has an openly specified structure in RFC 4155, so we can take some comfort there. Mbox essentially joins all the e-mails in a mailbox in a linear fashion. Both of these formats will be interpretable to most e-mail clients, and there are other tools available to read or convert from and to these formats.

Regardless of the presence of a specified structure for these formats, e-mail clients may elect to adjust the format structure, adding their own additions or modifications to the format. This is a difficult practice to fully work around, but it is atypical for a piece of software to so radically adjust a known format that it becomes unusable to other software familiar with that format. In other words, there is a reasonable expectation that if an e-mail client exports to a format like .mbox, that outputted file will be compatible with other software coded to work with .mbox.

There are numerous other ways to acquire e-mail. Mail clients often don't really store e-mail in a discrete format but, rather, manage the entirety of the e-mail in a database. Similarly, one could design a database to serve up acquired e-mails. However, this approach and similar advanced techniques require considerable planning and are usually tightly coupled with the access strategy. With .eml and .mbox, there is a reasonable assurance that, regardless of the access technology, you will have the content you acquired in a workable and complete format.

Now that you are familiar with the significant characteristics of e-mail, you can investigate more tailored tools for e-mail management and processing. One such tool we recommend starting with is the ePADD software package, hosted at Stanford University and developed with a number of collaborators. ePADD is open source software, runs on Windows and macOS machines, and contains four modules – Appraisal, Processing, Discovery and Delivery – for managing e-mail at your institution. As you may imagine from the module headings, the software offers functions for e-mail review, arrangement and description, sensitive information redaction, and an interface for user access to the e-mail archives. A previously acquired .mbox file can even be imported for use in the software.

Social media

If websites and e-mails are the stalwarts of the networked landscape, social media content is the younger upstart. Companies and services like Facebook, Twitter, Snapchat, Instagram and a host of others are wildly popular and often constitute the primary draw and output for many users online. The amount of content here is simply immense and the range of content type is similarly expansive. Social media content runs from the entirely mundane, such as images of lunches and innocuous selfies, to the controversial and provocative, to the instantly newsworthy and historic. What content falls into which category is largely a matter of your institution's collecting interest.

Common to all these services is proprietary technology. The Facebook wall and its posts, Twitter's tweets, Instagram's photos and feeds and innumerable others are all fundamentally closed technologies, regarded first and foremost as business assets and competitive advantages for the respective companies. As such, acquiring and subsequently preserving this content can be more challenging than for websites or e-mail. Nevertheless, the libraries, archives and museum fields have developed resources for just this task.

This area of research and development currently sees a great deal of change and flux, and, even if it did not, the number of social media services alone precludes us from diving in depth into acquisition. With that said, we want to point out a couple characteristics that run across all these services which will help you to decide on an acquisition strategy.

The first aspect to be aware of is exportability. Most social media services allow individual users to export their content in one format or other. That format may be HTML, images files, JavaScript Object Notation (JSON) exports, or some other structure. If exportability exists, your library or archives may be able to request the user to make such an export.

The second aspect is the existence (or not) of an application programming interface (API). An API is a mechanism produced by the company that allows users to programmatically interface with their service (the service being the 'application', in the nomenclature of the API). For example, Twitter provides a set of API instructions. These are agreed upon and publicly available commands that users can avail themselves of to search for tweets, download tweets and tweet content, receive user profile information and so on. API calls and requests need to be coded, so the technical imposition here is far higher than in the case of exportability. The upside, however, is that an API can allow you or your institution to systematically call for content from a service, while also allowing you to more easily move beyond capturing content produced by a single user.

There are of course other ways to capture content besides these service-sanctioned methods. While it isn't elegant or considered complete, you could take a screenshot. Even better, however, is the use of web crawlers or newer tools such as Webrecorder.io to capture dynamic social media content. Regardless of what method you choose, bear in mind that it is always best to closely consider what precisely you wish to capture – and why. This will give you the best chance of settling on a strategy that acquires what you are aiming for.

Accession

Accessioning an item or group of items is distinct from acquisition. An accession is a documentation of receipt and transfer of items, and typically ties the materials to an existing collection or declares the start of a new one. An accession usually records the legal nature of the transfer: deed of gift, deposit, purchase or other agreement. Accession processes are an acute need of archives, but they can be and are used in libraries as well, particularly in the case of published materials acquisitions (though the record of purchase may not always be referred to as an accession).

Here we want to focus on accessioning considerations for your born-digital material. If you are operating at the level of born-digital material purchasing, such as a set of GIS (geographical information system) data or business databases, the grouping for the accession record is fairly straightforward – whatever constitutes the content of the purchase is given an accession number and a collection name or is associated with a collection. If you are acquiring born-digital material first hand, the grouping level for an accession record can feature a little more for us to consider.

Let's say you are acquiring an image of a floppy disk. Here the accession record can be associated with the disk itself, tying the documentation to both the physical media and the digital bit-for-bit copy that stems from it. However, you may instead be acquiring a large group of floppy disks from a donor in a single transfer. In this case, it may be wise to have your accession record associate with this transfer instead, since it is a discrete donation of materials which you will want to be able to track and reference over time. The particular items in that accession can then receive further inventorying as you move into your processing workflow.

For born-digital content not coming to your institution on a physical carrier but, rather, over a network, the notion of a 'session' can be helpful. For example, you may initiate a crawl of a website. Crawling a website may take several hours or even longer, but once that session is complete, you can consider it a discrete transfer of materials for which an accession record is appropriate (note here again that a log of the session is especially helpful for a more complete accession record). Similarly, you may be using the Twitter API to acquire users' posts meeting certain criteria. That acquisition project may require only a single API call or request to the Twitter service, or it may require several calls where you are iterating the request or simply staggering the call over time. Depending on the completeness of the query or queries you can produce an accession for the single API call or for multiple, thematically or logically similar calls. You may need to make similar decisions if you are receiving e-mails from a donor which you will then save for your collection – where is the sensible dividing line for an accession record? That line may be at the end of each e-mail received or by some other grouping. Again, the idea of a session can help you to home in on where you want to assign the accession record.

Ingest

The final step we will discuss is ingesting born-digital materials into your repository. We use the term 'repository' loosely here, and simply mean the place or software that is designed as the final resting place of the content. For many institutions taking first steps into born-digital preservation, that final place will be a networked drive with a straightforward file and folder structure, typically under a set naming scheme, that houses the digital components of the institution's various collections. In this case, 'ingesting' is simply moving the content to the appropriate folder in this organization.

There is nothing intrinsically 'wrong' with this approach, though it does not scale well as files and collections grow to the hundreds and thousands. A basic file and folder system also lacks the ability to document the ingest itself, or any functionality to audit the contents over time. Many file systems do feature native abilities to check on the content stored on the system, though it is rare for that function to provide any clear reporting on those checks to the user.

If you are using a bare file and folder system to organize and manage your digital content, we recommend using a specification called BagIt to package your content as a final step. BagIt is an open packaging specification maintained by the Internet Engineering Task Force and is available as both a command line tool and as a GUI (dubbed Bagger), along with a number of other code formats. BagIt runs a scan on a targeted package (e.g. a collection of files constituting a website) and documents all files and folders in that target. It also runs a checksum algorithm (by default,

MD5) on each file in the package, producing that unique alphanumerical value for every file.

The collective output is a folder containing a plain text inventory of your content and a unique value listing for each file that can be recomputed to ensure validity and authenticity. This manifest is an excellent way to retain knowledge of what a group of born-digital content is supposed to contain. Provided you are able to do so, however, using a designated repository system or software is preferable to a bare file system. We will talk about repositories further in Chapter 5.

Conclusion

This has been an extensive chapter, but we have covered a great many processes in the field of born-digital preservation. You should now have good familiarity with:

- basic acquisition considerations and strategies for media on a physical carrier, including key concepts and use cases for digital forensics
- basic acquisition considerations and strategies for network-born media, including the key technologies and formats for websites and e-mail
- key technical aspects of social media services to consider when designing acquisition
- accessioning principles applied to born-digital media
- considerations for ingest and basic repository functions.

Further reading

Carrier, B. (2005) *File System Forensic Analysis*, Addison-Wesley.

We covered the basic principles and ideas in digital forensics here, but if you want to dig deeply into the forensics, Brian Carrier is an authoritative source who can guide you through the intricacies and hidden details of file systems you are likely to encounter.

OCLC Research (2017) 'Demystifying Born Digital Reports', www.oclc.org/research/publications/library/born-digital-reports.html.

OCLC (Online Computer Library Center) has produced excellent, brief reports on key starting points for born-digital materials handling, from workstation set-up to device capture and donor agreements. They are fantastic starting resources.

The Archivist's Guide to KryoFlux

If your journey into born-digital content leads you to the KryoFlux (and for many, it has), this will be a wonderful and potentially critical supplement to the terser, technical manual provided by the Software Preservation Society. Put together by practising professionals in the field, the guide orients new users of the device to the particular concerns of the archives and libraries fields – covering hardware and software set-up in more depth, along with floppy disk storage details, dealing with bad data or bad reads, reading log files and numerous other topics. This is an online resource in its final draft at the time of writing this book. The final version will be published here: www.dpconline.org/blog/kryoflux-manual and discoverable through Google search.

The IIPC (International Internet Preservation Consortium, http://netpreserve.org/.

If web archiving and site collecting is a major concern at your institution, IIPC can be a critical resource. The site hosts reports, case studies, tools and technologies, and working group activities – all centred on preserving the documentary record found online.

CHAPTER 4

Description

The digital order ignores the paper order's requirement that labels be smaller than the things they're labelling.

(David Weinberger, *Everything is Miscellaneous*, 2007, 19)

At best, describing born-digital content is complicated, but there are a few things you can consider when describing your content in either library or archival schema and systems that can smooth the way for you. As with every other aspect of collection and content management, the basic principles of description apply, but there are a few additional elements to consider when describing born-digital content.

In this chapter we'll explore some types of descriptive information that are particular to born-digital content, as well as various library and archives descriptive standards and systems that can be used to describe born-digital content. You will learn how various types of information about born-digital collections can be gathered to describe the content within different library and archives descriptive systems. We will discuss the general types of born-digital-specific information that you may want to compile, descriptive standards and element sets, and descriptive systems.

General fields and types of information

One of your first questions may be, 'what's different about born-digital description?' For the most part, you describe born-digital content in the same way as you would any other resource, but with a few exceptions. Let's take a minute to look at what types of descriptive information are generally the same across resources and where there may be differences.

Just about every library or archive resource has a title, some sort of date or range of dates and the name of an author or creator. In addition to these basic types of information, you should also think about collecting the following information.

- **Creation and revision dates or timestamps**. Unlike many analogue formats, creation and revision timestamp information is automatically generated and recorded for digital files. Much of this type of information is embedded within the digital file itself or in the surrounding file system of the media on which it is stored. In the latter case, collecting and storing this time and date information can be done automatically during ingest procedures. We discuss this type of metadata a little more in the 'Acquisition of born-digital material on a digital carrier' section of Chapter 3.
- **Fixity data**. As discussed in the previous chapter, fixity data are the checksums generated on ingest and are monitored for changes over time. This type of data is entirely new to library and archives resource description, but is imperative to collect for digital content.
- **File types and formats**. Recording the file type or file format of your digital content is important for knowing what kind of software is necessary to meaningfully render the file. Services such as the UK National Archives' PRONOM technical registry provide simple file format identifiers that can be recorded in some descriptive schemas and systems. The UK National Archives actually provides its own free tool, DROID (Digital Record Object Identification), to identify files on a local machine.
- **Rendering software**. In addition to knowing the file formats of your digital content, it's also useful to record information about what types of software one will need to render the file. Some of this information may seem obvious to us now but, as technology changes so quickly over time, the knowledge of which software is needed to render particular file formats may become obscured. Collecting this information now will take some of the guesswork out of this in the future.
- **Hardware**. In some cases it is useful to record information about any hardware that is (or was) necessary to provide access to the digital content. With current and more ubiquitous types of digital content, this may not seem like an issue, since the internet often acts as the common denominator for use and access. With older and more obscure formats, there may be very specific hardware requirements for providing access. Like recording rendering software information, recording information about hardware requirements will save users extra guesswork down the road, and regardless of the current mode

of access for the content (such as emulation), this information can serve as a historical note on how the content *was* accessed for users at the time.

- **Physical media information**. It may be useful to collect information about the type of physical media on which the content arrived and/or is currently stored. This information can include the type of disk or drive, the formatting of the disk or drive and, if relevant, any writing that appears on labels or the media itself. Since some important contextual information may exist on the exterior of the media, you may also consider taking a photograph of the disk or drive itself and maintain that as linked metadata.
- **Linked or associated files**. Many digital files are only a component of larger, complex digital objects. In cases where there are multi-document files, linked pages, back-end databases or linked executable code it is important to record the relationships between a digital file and other files or digital objects. Failing to do so could at best damage the context of the content, and at worst make the file unrenderable.
- **Access codes and encryption keys**. In some rare cases, you will acquire files that require a code to access the content. This may be because of a piece of software blocking access or because the content is actually encrypted (i.e. systematically scrambled) and requires the encryption key to decrypt it. In more rare cases, you will actually have access to the code or encryption key. When you have digital content that requires this information, you should definitely record it if possible.
- **Copyrights and licensing**. Recording and sharing copyrights and licensing information is typical for most types of library and archives content; however, born-digital content may present different challenges here, so it's useful to be aware of these differences and document them accordingly. Copyrights and licensing is covered in more detail in Chapter 6.
- **Personally identifying information (PII) and other private information**. Acquisitions of digital content are much more likely to contain private information and are much easier to share and transmit across the globe. If there is known PII in the files, it is important to record the fact that this information exists so that decisions can be made about redaction efforts and access restrictions.
- **Conservation treatments**. These entail any activities that alter any

aspect of the nature of the original born-digital object in order to preserve one's ability to access it over time. The most prevalent of these activities are normalisation of the digital object to a pre-determined file format and general migration of the digital object to another file format to avoid access issues related to potential file format obsolescence.

Your job will be to consider each of these new types of information when planning to describe born-digital content. There aren't perfect solutions for all of these types of information yet, but we will explore how various existing descriptive standards and systems can be used to address these needs.

Descriptive standards and element sets

Here we will cover some of the descriptive standards, schemas and languages and dig into some of the ways they may be used to describe born-digital content. This won't cover all description possibilities comprehensively, but should give you an idea of how you can define your own practices. We will look at description in libraries and archives and some general description options. We are working from the assumption that you have a basic understanding of descriptive practices in libraries or archives and so will be building on that beginning level of knowledge to learn how to use or adapt existing element sets and descriptive standards to describe born-digital resources.

In our experience, a number of related terms and phrases have been used in multiple ways and sometimes interchangeably. In this book, we'll focus on descriptive standards and element sets. For our purposes, we define *descriptive standards* as the rules and guidelines that define how the fields in these element sets should be filled in. *Element sets* are the list of fields for which you provide the values. We will look at descriptive standards and element sets specific to bibliographic and archival content, and at some that are used in broader contexts.

Bibliographic descriptive standards

Bibliographic descriptive standards have been used for many decades to describe books and other similar printed material. These standards have been adapted for audio and visual materials and most recently they have been adapted to describe electronic and even born-digital content. We will review the Anglo-American Cataloging Rules (AACR) and Machine Readable Cataloging (MARC), Resources Description and Access (RDA) and BIBFRAME, and the International Standard Bibliographic Description (ISBD) and International Standard Bibliographic Description for Electronic Resources (ISBD (ER)).

AACR and MARC

Up until recently, one of the most common sets of rules for cataloging bibliographic resources has been the AACR2 (Anglo-American Cataloging Rules, 2nd Edition) and the related MARC standards for the 21st century (MARC 21). A large portion of library and archives resources are described using these sets of rules and standards, including born-digital content. While the standard was officially superseded by the RDA standard, many existing resources are still described using AACR2/MARC rules and formatting. Considering this, let's take a look at some of the specific fields you can use to describe certain aspects of your born-digital resources.

You certainly won't find all of the fields you need to thoroughly describe your resources in this set of rules. In addition to your typical descriptive information such as title, author and creation date, you will be able to indicate somewhere that the resource is a 'computer file' or an 'electronic resource', which is indicated by a code 'm' in the 'Type of Record' field in the leader area. Also in the leader area, you can indicate the type of computer file by using one of the following codes.

- a Numeric data
- b Computer program
- c Representational
- d Document
- e Bibliographic data
- f Font
- g Game
- h Sound
- i Interactive multimedia
- j Online system or service
- m Combination
- u Unknown
- z Other

In the 007 field, you have a number of options for defining specific pieces of information about your resource.

- $a Category of material
- $b Specific material designation
- $d Color
- $e Dimensions
- $j Antecedent/Source
- $f Sound
- $g Image bit depth
- $h File formats
- $i Quality assurance target(s)
- $k Level of compression
- $l Reformatting quality

The 856 field allows you to document URLs and other electronic locations for access using the following sub-fields.

- # No information provided
- 0 E-mail
- 1 FTP
- 2 Remote login (Telnet)
- 3 Dial-up
- 4 HTTP
- 7 Source specified in subfield $2

There is also detailed information in the standards about how to best format URLs, taking into consideration diacritics – such as accents and tildes over letters – and other special characters. Additionally, the following subfields are available to record more detailed information such as password and logon information as well as file format and compression information.

- a Host name
- b Access number
- c Compression information
- d Path
- f Electronic name
- g Uniform Resource Name [obsolete]

- h Processor of request
- i Instruction
- j BPS
- k Password
- l Logon
- m Contact for access assistance
- n Name of location of host in subfield $a
- o Operating system
- p Port
- q Electronic format type
- r Settings
- s File size
- t Terminal emulation
- u Uniform Resource Identifier
- v Hours access method available
- w Record control number
- x Nonpublic note
- y Link text
- z Public note
- 2 Source of access
- 3 Materials specified

These are just a few examples of how you can use some of the existing AACR2 and MARC fields for born-digital content. There are many other fields you can explore to this end. A number of these options are described in detail in the *Rules and Tools for Cataloging Internet Resources Trainee Manual*, described in the further reading section below.

RDA and BIBFRAME

RDA succeeded AACR2 as a descriptive cataloguing standard over the course of 2010. RDA is based upon a few key conceptual models that preceded it: the Functional Requirements for Bibliographic Records (FRBR), Functional Requirements for Authority Data (FRAD) and Functional Requirements for Subject Authority Data (FRSAD), which are all maintained by the International Federation of Library Associations and Institutions (IFLA). RDA is similar to AACR2, though there are some nominal and some more substantial differences between the two. For example, RDA moves away from the usage of abbreviations, and some of the terms for physical descriptions have shifted, such as from 'sound recordings' to 'audio recordings'. RDA is also designed to support linked data practices, to function better as an international standard and to better describe a wider range of resource types than AACR2. You can learn more by reviewing the RDA-related resources provided by the Library of Congress, as described in the further reading section below.

BIBFRAME is a descriptive model for bibliographic resources finalised in 2013. It is designed to work well with RDA, and uses many RDA elements in its vocabulary, while also aiming to replace the MARC standard as a shared method of bibliographic description. BIBFRAME is a good example of how a descriptive standard like RDA adjusts the expectations for description.

ISBD

ISBD was developed by the International Meeting of Cataloguing Experts, organized by the IFLA Committee on Cataloguing in Copenhagen in 1969. A number of related standards grew from this core, including ISBD (ER), which was superseded by the 2011 ISBD Consolidated Edition. The ISBD standard functions very similarly to AACR2 and RDA, but with a few adjustments to make it suitable in various international descriptive environments.

There are additional fields and notations that were consolidated and updated from ISBD (ER) that can be used to address the needs of electronic resources and that function well for born-digital content. The greatest difference exists in the media type distinctions, where you can note either that the resource is in electronic format or that various types of media like audio and video resources are in digital form. You will most likely document more individual format and technical specifications using the elements described in section 7 'Notes on the content form and media type area and for special types of material'. The following subsections in section 7 of the ISBD may be useful to you.

- 7.0.4. System requirements (Electronic resources)
- 7.0.5. Mode of access (Electronic resources)
- 7.3.1.3 Digital cartographic resources
- 7.9 Notes on the issue, part, iteration, etc., that forms the basis of the description; specifically for remote-access electronic resources.

Archives

Like bibliographic description standards, there are also a number of descriptive standards designed specifically for archival content, with several variations for different geographic regions. The General International Standard Archival Description (ISAD(G)) is akin to ISBD in that it is the broadest standard designed to cover the needs of the whole international community, not just some isolated regions. RAD was created and is used primarily in Canada; Describing Archives: a Content Standard (DACS) is predominantly used in the USA and the Manual of Archival Description (MAD) is a UK-centric archival description standard. They all function in more or less the same way, but with some minor, regional variations.

(ISAD(G))

The ISAD(G) 2nd Edition was published by the International Council on Archives and is available in 15 languages. This standard outlines all of the typical archival description fields such as title, creator, dates, extent, biographical/administrative history, level of description and system of arrangement. There are very few fields included in this standard that address born-digital specific descriptive needs. The one pertinent field, however, is 3.4.4 'Physical characteristics and technical requirements'. This field has historically been used to indicate technical requirements for viewing analogue materials, but it can certainly be put to use in describing the technical needs for accessing born-digital content.

RAD

Last updated in 2009, RAD is a Canadian archival description standard. It follows many of the same principles of archival description delineated in ISAD(G), but presents additional information on specific resource types such as sound recordings, moving images and 'records in electronic form'. For the most part, the chapter explaining treatment of electronic records follows the same guidelines as other resources. One primary difference is that in section 9.5B2, under 'Extent of descriptive unit', the authors permit the optional description of a digital extent of the unit being described, in Arabic numerals; their example being '5 GB of photographs'. Overall, this standard provides extensive options and guidance for describing digital content. It ofers additional parameters for describing the following digitally specific attributes.

- 9.5B3. Number of physical carriers. Examples:
  - 2 CD-ROMs (textual records)
  - 1 zip disk (96 MB)
  - 1 computer disk
- 9.5C1. Additional notes on sound (sd) and or color (col). Examples:
- 1 TB of cartographic material
- 1 computer disc : sd., col.
- 9.5C2. Notes on number of sides used, recording density, sectoring, storage capacity, tracks. Examples:
  - 1 computer disk : sd., col., single sided, single density, soft sectored
  - 2 computer reels : 6250 bpi
- 9.5D1. For physical dimensions of items described in 9.5B3. Example:
  - 1 computer disk ; 9 x 9 cm
- 9.5E1. For details about accompanying material. Examples:
  - 5 GB of photographs : col. + 1 poster
  - 15 MB (1 map) : col. + 1 pamphlet
- 9.7D2. System description. Description of the hardware and software requirements of the system necessary for access
- 9.7D2a. System name and developer
- 9.7D2b. Hardware
- 9.7D2c. Operating system
- 9.7D2d. Network or multi-user configuration
- 9.7D2e. System security and access
- 9.7D2f. Programming language.
- 9.7D2g. Software/application capabilities
- 9.7D2h. System documentation
- 9.7D2i. System milestones which consist of major events affecting the design and operation of the system
- 9.7D2j. Location of system software
- 9.8B1a. System requirements for access. Examples:
  - System requirements: 48K RAM, Apple Disk II with controller, col. monitor (Computer file requires colour monitor for display)
  - System requirements: RTI Series 500 CD-ROM DataDrive (File is available on CD-ROM) 9.8B1b. Remote access. If the unit being described is available via remote access, make a note indicating relevant information needed to access it. If appropriate, give mode of access, site, and path, Uniform Resource Locator (URL), or other international standard designation for this information.

- 9.8B10b. Conservation. Make notes on any specific conservation treatment. Example:
  - Computer files migrated by the National Archives of Canada from original word-processing software (MICOM) to WordPerfect, version 4.2 to maintain readability of data. Technical specifications of the migration are filed with the printed documentation
- 9.8B14. Arrangement. Example:
  - When the records were transferred to the Archives, the computer files were arranged in subdirectories which reflect the original work stations from which they came
- 9.8B16b. Availability of other formats. Examples:
  - Also available in printed form and in microform
  - Issued also for IBM PC and PC-compatible hardware
- 9.8B17. Restrictions on access, use, reproduction, and publication. Examples:
  - Restricted: Contains respondent's name and telephone numbers. Must be anonymized before dissemination
  - Researchers must sign an undertaking that they will not reveal information about living persons without their written consent.

You can learn more details about these and other RAD description guidelines via the RAD documentation described in the further reading section below.

DACS

As the US implementation of ISAD(G), DACS, 2nd Edition is the most commonly implemented archival description standard in the USA. Compared with the Canadian RAD standard, DACS contains some but not quite as much direct guidance for describing digital content.

Under field 2.5.7 'Multiple Statements of Extent', the authors do provide the example of '52 megabytes (1,180 computer files)' and '0.5 linear feet (51 floppy discs, 5 Zip discs, 3 CD-ROMs)'. They also provide this guidance for 'Statements of Extent for Electronic Records' under section 2.5.10: 'Electronic records may be described in terms of size (kilobytes, megabytes, gigabytes) or in terms of structure (digital files, directories, items, etc.). If desired, both may be used.' They include the following examples.

- 700 Megabytes
- 3 file directories containing 48 PDF files
- 23 digital files (1 Gigabyte)
- approximately 275 digital image and audio files (12.4 GB) on
- 1 portable hard drive.

Additionally under section 2.5.1, they state: 'Optionally, descriptions of electronic records may include file format type as well as size. The file format type is normally the file name extension (.doc, .pdf, .ppt, etc.). This is especially recommended where the description includes a link directly to the record.' Section 4.3 provides some guidance on describing access restrictions that exist due to technical requirements. Section 4.3.6 provides specific guidance for describing technical requirements for digital content, with the addition of the following example.

- The Personnel Master File contains fourteen rectangular flat files stored in standard label EBCDIC. The files contain numeric and character data. The files are stored on fourteen reels of tape at 6250 bpi. The data can be manipulated using a common statistical package. Tape copies are in standard label EBCDIC format. Floppy disk copies are in ASCII format. System requirements: 48K RAM; Apple Disk II with controller; colour monitor required to view this file.

Section 7.1.4 specifies the guidance for describing any conservation treatment performed on digital files such as migration or logical re-formatting. For example:

- Computer files migrated by the National Archives of Canada from original word-processing software (MICOM) to WordPerfect version 4.2 to maintain readability of data. Technical specifications of the migration are filed with the printed documentation.

More information on DACS descriptive guidance may be found in the DACS resources described in the further reading section below.

MAD, UK

MAD provides overall descriptive guidance and rules for descriptive element sets for archival description in the UK. Even as early as the 1989 edition, MAD provided rules for elements specifically designed for machine-readable content. Specifically, section 25.5 of MAD provides these rules for data elements for machine-readable archives. Elements of interest are the following.

- 25.5B1 Production, sub-section on copyright
- 25.5B2 Content sub-area. In this element, you may record detailed information about the form of the materials, i.e. the types of the data file (bibliographic, text, graphics, numeric, etc.); information about the operating system, program language; as well as detailed information about complex digital objects and how associated files are linked.
- 25.5B3 Physical description. This element can include information about the size of the digital file in terms of kilobytes or lines of code, the type of physical medium, and other defining characteristics such as density, number of tracks, bits per inch (bpi), etc.
- 25.5B4 Technical description. This element includes information about memory requirements, software language dependence, and the peripheral equipment (microphones, keyboards, screens, speakers, etc.) required to access the materials.
- 25.5C Management information. This element includes information about conservation actions taken to preserve the materials, but can also include other administrative information like process history, subsequent accession information, access conditions, and service charges.

For full explanation of these and other element rules and guidance, you can purchase the manual, cited fully in the further reading section below.

General element sets

Growing out of the sometimes limiting and sometimes overly varying standards discussed above are a number of more general descriptive element sets that address a range of needs in the field. We will discuss two of the more common element sets – Dublin Core and PREMIS – and how each of them may be used for born-digital content.

Dublin Core

The Dublin Core metadata element set is known most famously as an effort to create an incredibly versatile element set that could be used in almost any resource description setting. The resulting element set is comprised of 15 core elements: Title, Creator, Subject, Description, Publisher, Contributor, Date, Type, Format, Identifier, Source, Language, Relation, Coverage and Rights. While there is little direct guidance for describing digital content, a number of these elements can be adapted to describe born-digital resources. For example, the Format and Type elements can be used to indicate file format and resource type, respectively.

PREMIS

You may have noticed that fixity data has not yet been addressed by any of the descriptive standards or element sets. One could argue that it is one of the most important pieces of information about your digital content, which you should collect and regularly check. Luckily for all of us, the PREMIS preservation metadata set was created to collect this and just about every other type of data you would need about your born-digital content. The PREMIS metadata dictionary is about 280 pages of densely packed guidelines for describing digital content, so outlining all of the useful elements here is well outside the scope of this book. To describe it briefly, the standard is divided into five conceptual entities: Object (digital object), Environment, Event, Agent and Rights Statement. Within each of these entities are sets of metadata elements used to describe different aspects of a digital object, revolving around its environment, rights associated with it, events in which it is involved and the agents that take part in these events.

Some important elements to review in the context of this discussion are the following.

- 1.5.2 Fixity, where you will store and check the checksum information for your digital object.
- 1.5.4 Format, where you will store information identifying the file format of your digital object, typically in the form of a PRONOM file format registry number, as we discuss in Chapter 5 ('A note on file formats').
- 1.5.6 Inhibitors, where you will collect information about functions that may inhibit access to your digital content such as encryption, and

the means by which you can bypass the inhibitor, such as an encryption key or access code.
- 1.7.2 Storage Medium, where you keep information about the physical medium on which the digital content is stored.
- 1.9 Environment Function, used to describe the 'environment' or the software and hardware necessary to render the digital resource.
- 1.13 Relationship, where you record information about the digital object's relationship with other digital objects, and which is particularly important in documenting the relationships within a complex digital object.
- 2.2 Event Type and all of the associated Event entity elements, which are important for describing conservation actions like migration, but can also be used to record fixity checks, ingest actions and validation.

These are just a few of the very many options you have at your disposal in this standard. PREMIS metadata definitely isn't for the faint of heart, but it is well worth the effort to get to know it. We highly recommend that you spend some time reading through the narrative and element definitions in the data dictionary resource listed in the further reading section below.

A comparison across standards and element sets

After reviewing these descriptive standards and element sets individually, we can take some time to compare each of them against our list of the general types of information that we would ideally be able to collect about our born-digital content. If you take a look at Table 4.1 on the next page, you will see that none of the standards by itself provides the ability to collect all of the information we may need. Some, like RAD and PREMIS, provide the mechanism for you to collect most of the types of information you may need. You may also be in a position where your institution is already using one standard, like AACR2 or DACS, and you can start there and supplement with additional standards to fill in the gaps.

Descriptive systems

Descriptive standards and element sets are usually implemented within various systems designed to host library and archival descriptive content. A number of these systems are designed to support particular standards and element sets, and some are designed to be flexible enough to support multiple, separate and sometimes combined standards and sets. The more

Table 4.1 *Comparison of born-digital information needs across descriptive standards and element sets*

	AACR2	RDA	ISBD	ISAD(G)	RAD	DACS	MAD	DC	PREMIS
Dates/ Timestamps	X	X	X	X	X	X	X	X	X
Fixity									X
File types	X	X		X	X	X	X	X	X
Software			X	X	X	X	X	X	X
Hardware			X	X	X	X	X		X
Physical media	X	X	X	X	X	X	X	X	X
Linked Files				X	X	X	X	X	X
Access Codes									X
Rights	X	X	X	X	X	X	X	X	X
PII					X				
Conservation					X	X	X		X

flexible systems are the most ideal, since, as we discussed previously, no one standard or set supports all of the types of information needed to adequately describe born-digital content.

Bibliographic descriptive systems

There are dozens of bibliographic descriptive systems on the market, most commonly in the form of integrated library systems. Some of the more prevalent systems are Millennium, Alma, OCLC Worldshare and Koha. These systems are built around the current bibliographic descriptive standards of MARC 21 and RDA and leave little room for including descriptive fields outside of these standards. If born-digital content is described in these types of system, it is usually at a very basic level, and often linked to another system that can provide deeper information about the content.

Archival description systems

Like bibliographic descriptive systems, archival description systems are primarily built around archival descriptive standards. Fortunately, however, most of the current archival description systems have built in capabilities to include information specific to born-digital content. For example, while the core of ArchivesSpace is built around DACS, it has an entire content type devoted to digital objects. Within this content type are fields for file formats, checksums and event data such as migrations. Similarly AtoM is built around the ISAD(G) descriptive standard, but is designed to also support RAD, DACS, Dublin Core and the Metadata Object Description Standard (MODS).

Digital repositories

There are also systems designed specifically to collect, describe and provide access to digital content, commonly known as digital repositories. There are quite a few different digital repository systems available, among them, CONTENTdm, Digital Commons, DSpace, EPrints, Hydra, Islandora and RODA. Unlike systems that are built specifically for describing content and which are built around existing descriptive standards, digital repositories tend to lean more toward being descriptive standard agnostic, and provide flexible interfaces in which you can decide on the fields that are best suited for your case.

Digital preservation systems

There is software designed for collecting digital content that is more geared toward preserving the content and less focused on access. A number of digital preservation systems are available that fit this description, such as Archivematica, Preservica and Rosetta. In these systems, the descriptive information collected for the digital content is focused on digital preservation needs, and so more often they collect data as outlined in the PREMIS descriptive standard.

Use cases

We have a few examples of how you can put some of this into practice. Figure 4.1 overleaf demonstrates how one might describe a floppy disk using the MARC description standard. Figure 4.2 demonstrates how a born-digital image can be described in the ArchivesSpace descriptive system using DACS with some additional elements found in PREMIS. Lastly, in Figure 4.3 you can see some PREMIS metadata for a born-digital image marked up in eXtensible Markup Language (XML).

Type	m	ELvl		Srce	c	Audn		Ctrl		Lang	eng
BLvl	m	Form	q	GPub				MRec		Ctry	cau
Desc	i	File	g			DtSt	t	Dates	1990	,	1990

007			c ǂb j ǂd c ǂe o ǂf a
040			STF ǂb eng ǂe rda ǂc STF ǂd STF ǂd OCLCF
042			pcc
090			ǂb
049			CODA
245	0	0	Strike aces / ǂc Accolade.
246	1		ǂi Title on container: ǂa Strike aces : ǂb international bombing competition.
250			Ver. 1.2.
250			[IBM PC, XT, AT, Tandy].
264		1	San Jose, CA : ǂb Accolade, ǂc [1990].
264		4	ǂc ©1990
300			4 computer discs : ǂb sound, color ; ǂc 5 1/4 in. + ǂe 1 volume (63 pages : illustrations ; 18 cm)
336			two-dimensional moving image ǂ2 rdacontent
336			computer program ǂ2 rdacontent
337			computer ǂ2 rdamedia
338			computer disc ǂ2 rdacarrier
344			digital $b optical $2 rda
380			Video game.
500			Accompanied by a code wheel.
538			System requirements: IMB PC, XT, AT + 100% compatibles with 512K memory; Tandy 1000 series, 3000, 4000 with 640 K memory; VGA, EGA, CGA, Herc MGA, or Tandy 16 color graphics.
538			Disc characteristics: 5 1/4 floppy disk.
500			Title from disc labels.
505	0		VGA disc -- CGS disk -- EGA/Tandy disc -- [Hercules disc].
520			"Fly one of 6 lethal strike aircraft against 7 international interceptors. Embark on 16 precision bombing missions or create unlimited attack runs with the "Mission Design" feature."--Container.
650		0	Bombers ǂv Computer games.
650		0	Bombing, Aerial ǂv Computer games.

Figure 4.1 *An OCLC MARC record describing floppy disks*

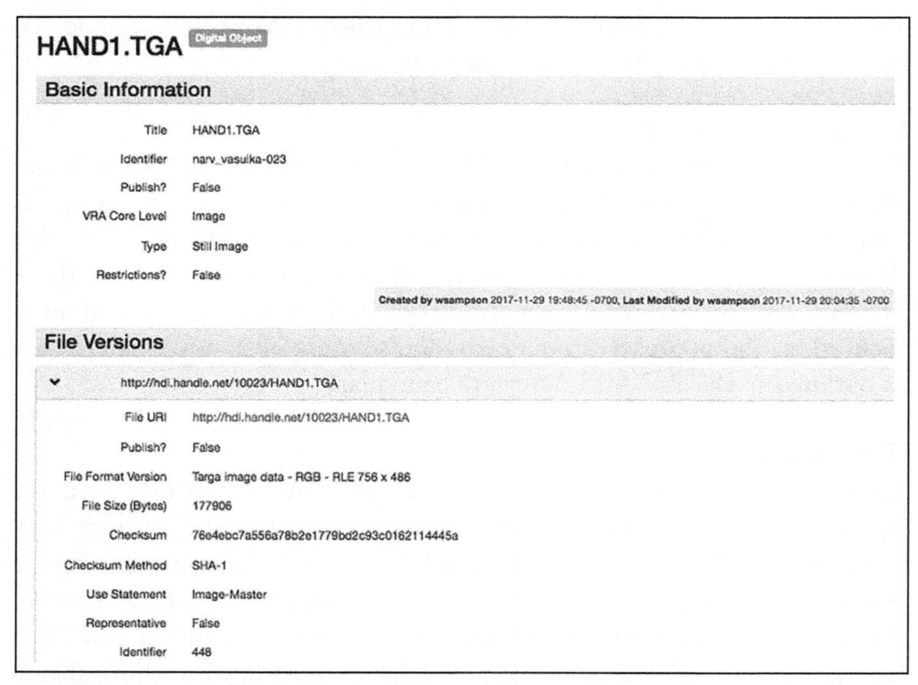

HAND1.TGA Digital Object

Basic Information

Title	HAND1.TGA
Identifier	narv_vasulka-023
Publish?	False
VRA Core Level	Image
Type	Still Image
Restrictions?	False

Created by wsampson 2017-11-29 19:48:45 -0700, **Last Modified by** wsampson 2017-11-29 20:04:35 -0700

File Versions

http://hdl.handle.net/10023/HAND1.TGA

File URI	http://hdl.handle.net/10023/HAND1.TGA
Publish?	False
File Format Version	Targa image data - RGB - RLE 756 x 486
File Size (Bytes)	177906
Checksum	76e4ebc7a556a78b2e1779bd2c93c0162114445a
Checksum Method	SHA-1
Use Statement	Image-Master
Representative	False
Identifier	448

Figure 4.2 *Screenshot of a digital object described in ArchivesSpace using DACS with additional digital object specific fields*

```
<?xml version="1.0" encoding="UTF-8"?>
<premis xmlns="info:lc/xmlns/premis-v2"
xmlns:xsi="http://www.w3.org/2001/XMLSchema-instance"
version="2.0">
<!— premis file object —>
<object xsi:type="file">
 <objectIdentifier>
  <objectIdentifierType>URI</objectIdentifierType>
 <objectIdentifierValue>/tmp/4649_HAND1.TGA</objectIdentifierValue>
 </objectIdentifier>
 <objectCharacteristics>
  <compositionLevel>0</compositionLevel>
  <fixity>
        <messageDigestAlgorithm>MD5</messageDigestAlgorithm>

     <messageDigest>fcac3a82399df90445b6a8adbb38774b</messageDigest>
        <messageDigestOriginator>Archive</messageDigestOriginator>
       </fixity>
       <fixity>
        <messageDigestAlgorithm>SHA-1</messageDigestAlgorithm>
        <messageDigest>76e4ebc7a556a78b2e1779bd2c93c0162114445a
        </messageDigest>
        <messageDigestOriginator>Archive</messageDigestOriginator>
       </fixity>
       <size>177906</size>
       <format>
        <formatDesignation>
         <formatName>Truevision TGA Bitmap</formatName>
         <formatVersion>1.0</formatVersion>
        </formatDesignation>
        <formatRegistry>

     <formatRegistryName>http://www.nationalarchives.gov.uk/pronom
     </formatRegistryName>
         <formatRegistryKey>x-fmt/367</formatRegistryKey>
        </formatRegistry>
       </format>
      </objectCharacteristics>
      <originalName>HAND1.TGA</originalName>
       <linkingEventIdentifier>
      <linkingEventIdentifierType>URI</linkingEventIdentifierType>
      <linkingEventIdentifierValue>1</linkingEventIdentifierValue>
```


Figure 4.3 *PREMIS metadata for a TARGA image of a hand*

```
</linkingEventIdentifier>
</object>
<!— premis bitstream object —>
<!— premis event —>
<event>
<eventIdentifier>
 <eventIdentifierType>URI</eventIdentifierType>
 <eventIdentifierValue>1</eventIdentifierValue>
</eventIdentifier>
<eventType>describe</eventType>
<eventDateTime>2017-11-29T20:57:23-05:00</eventDateTime>
<eventDetail>format identified</eventDetail>
<eventOutcomeInformation>
 <eventOutcome>success</eventOutcome>
</eventOutcomeInformation>
<linkingAgentIdentifier>
<linkingAgentIdentifierType>URI</linkingAgentIdentifierType>
<linkingAgentIdentifierValue>info:fda/daitss/description/v2.4.
1</linkingAgentIdentifierValue>
</linkingAgentIdentifier>
<linkingObjectIdentifier>
<linkingObjectIdentifierType>URI</linkingObjectIdentifierType>
<linkingObjectIdentifierValue>/tmp/4649_HAND1.TGA
</linkingObjectIdentifierValue>
</linkingObjectIdentifier>
</event>
<!— premis agent —><Agent><AgentIdentifier>
 <agentIdentifierType>URI</agentIdentifierType>
<agentIdentifierValue>info:fda/daitss/description/v2.4.1
</agentIdentifierValue>
</agentIdentifier><AgentName>Format Description
Service</agentName><AgentType>Web
Service</agentType><AgentNote>built with JHOVE 1.11, DROID 3.0
with DROID signature file version 67.</agentNote>
</agent>
</premis>
```


Figure 4.3 *Continued*

Conclusion

It is rare that an institution uses only one system to collect, preserve and provide access to its born-digital content. You will select or may have already selected a suite of descriptive standards and systems to manage your content and so you will be able to collect most, if not all, of the information you need. The important thing to remember is that the more information you collect about your born-digital content, the greater the probability that you will be able to preserve and provide access to that content. Collecting and managing metadata about your content is very time intensive, and is often the most expensive and resource-intensive part of your workflow. It's a fine balance to manage, but one you can revise and refine over time.

After reading this chapter you should know more about:

- The types of information you should collect about born-digital content
- How born-digital content is addressed in different descriptive standards and element sets.

Further reading

We share a few more resources in this chapter than usual to make sure to direct you to all of the available descriptive standards we discuss in this chapter.

Bunn, Jenny (2016) *Best Guess Guidelines for Cataloging Born Digital Material*, Archives and Records Association of the UK and Ireland.

In many ways much of what current library and archives professionals do with their born-digital content is best guesses, and so the title of this online resource is apropos. The resource itself provides detailed information on describing archival born-digital content.

Canadian Committee on Archival Description (2008) *Rules for Archival Description (RAD)*, Canadian Council of Archives.

This publication provides the rules for describing archival material; primarily used in Canada.

Dublin Core Metadata Initiative (2012) *Dublin Core Metadata Element Set, Version 1.1: Reference Description*, ASIS&T.

The element set famously created in Dublin, Ohio with the aim of creating the metadata set to end all metadata sets. The 16 core elements and their variations are all described in the document.

International Council on Archives Sub-Committee on Descriptive Standards (2011) *ISAD(G): General International Standard Archival Description, 2nd edn*, International Council on Archives.

The ICA provides its guidelines for description in 15 languages: Croatian, Czech, Dutch, English, French, German, Greek, Hebrew, Polish, Portuguese, Romanian, Russian, Serbian, Spanish, and Welsh.

International Federation of Library Associations, Cataloguing Section and ISBD Review Group (2011) *International Standard Bibliographic Description (ISBD), consolidated edition*, De Gruyter Saur.

The consolidated edition merges the texts of the six specialised ISBDs (for books, maps, serials, sound recordings, computer files and other electronic resources, etc.) into a single text. Of particular interest, of course, will be the chapters on computer files and other electronic resources.

Library of Congress (2017) *Bibliographic Framework Initiative*, www.loc.gov/bibframe/, Library of Congress.

This Library of Congress web page is the central location for the most important information about BIBFRAME. It includes description of the model and the related vocabulary, additional documentation, news, training materials and community information.

Library of Congress (2017) *Resource Description and Access (RDA): information and resources in preparation for RDA*, www.loc.gov/aba/rda/, Library of Congress.

This Library of Congress web page is the central location for the most important information about RDA. It includes the core element sets, additional documentation, news, training materials and community information.

Miller, S. J. (2008) *Rules and Tools for Cataloging Internet Resources*, Library of Congress.

The materials on this Library of Congress web page include an extensive trainee manual and the accompanying slides that provide detailed guidance for describing resources that are accessible on the world wide web using AACR2 and MARC 21.

PREMIS Editorial Committee (2015) *PREMIS Data Dictionary for Preservation Metadata, version 3.0*, Library of Congress.

This document provides the guidelines for describing elements that relate to the preservation of digital objects.

Proctor, M. and Cook, M. (2016) *Manual of Archival Description*, Routledge.

This manual provides the rules for describing archival material; primarily used in the UK. Of all of the descriptive rule sets, this is the only one not openly available online.

Riley, J. (2017) *Understanding Metadata: what is metadata, and what is it for?* National Information Standards Organization (NISO).

This is a fantastic general primer on metadata, written by Jenn Riley who created the famous *Seeing Standards: a visualization of the metadata universe* (2009–10), which is another invaluable resource.

Technical Subcommittee on Describing Archives: a Content Standard (2013) *Describing Archives: a Content Standard (DACS), 2nd edn,* Society of American Archivists.

This document provides the rules for describing archival material; primarily used in the USA.

Timms, K. (2013) *The Devil Is in the Details: describing born-digital records using the Rules for Archival Description,* lecture presented at the Society of American Archivist conference, http://files.archivists.org/conference/nola2013/materials/701-TimmsA.pdf.

Presents an overview of challenges that arise when attempting to implement RAD for electronic resources in various born-digital content scenarios.

CHAPTER 5

Digital preservation storage and strategies

> Let us save what remains: not by vaults and locks which fence them from the public eye and use in consigning them to the waste of time, but by such a multiplication of copies, as shall place them beyond the reach of accident.
>
> (Thomas Jefferson, *Letter to Ebenezer Hazard*, 1791)

The best practices of preservation, digital or otherwise, are a constantly developing subject in libraries, archives and museums. Along with this dynamism, there are a range of practices that can be listed under the heading of 'preservation' – the term can simultaneously describe the entirety of the work of an archivist and refer to specific tasks centred on the future legibility and usability of a document or object. The Multilingual Archival Terminology project features several explanations of the term, but this chapter will take the following definition as the most germane for our discussion: 'The whole of the principles, policies, rules and strategies aimed at prolonging the existence of an object by maintaining it in a condition suitable for use, either in its original format or in a more persistent format, while leaving intact the object's intellectual form.' Note here that preservation is an ongoing act – objects are kept in a state of use not in a single performance, but from continuous care.

We will be primarily focused on the preservation of groups of objects from an organizational perspective. For example, what policies can you put together to describe how your organization takes care of digital objects? What can you promise, and what can you not? What strategies will you use for storage of the objects, and what are the best practices for long-term retention of that digital data? All these concerns describe the work of preservation – again, the act of keeping from harm – at a scale larger than the individual digital object, accession or collection.

A note on acquisition

Digital objects are often born into environments which are unstable or fluctuating. Think of a comment in a user forum appending an online article; a Facebook wall entry you spotted the other week; or a tweet from a journalist one month ago. Or even more generally, recall a site you liked, an old software program located on a floppy disk or an e-mail you sent to a friend a few years ago. In all these cases, objects are created in environments built for their use and transmission, not their preservation and organization. Floppy disks are for sticking into floppy drives or setting in a plastic case on your desk; tweets are for reading in a Twitter timeline, reposting to others or favouriting; while websites, online commentary and Facebook material are conceived of first and foremost for consumption, sharing and linking – not retention.

Naturally, physical materials exhibit the same problem, but born-digital objects suffer acutely in this area because digital environments are typically more volatile than physical environments. Websites revamp their aesthetic and jettison old material, or the site itself goes down. Floppies become so outmoded that their contents are entirely opaque to any non-specialist. Tweets and other social media are deleted by their users, or become so old that the service moves them aside from quick recall, often requiring custom coding to recover them. Comments are served by a separate service from the site they are located on, and are problematic to the usual site acquisition tools – and so on.

In these cases, the simple act of acquiring the material itself, through whatever means, is often the single greatest stride in its preservation. If you can copy a tweet from your timeline, a Facebook post from the wall or a site from the servers that host it, you may have made the largest step to ensuring its future availability. We'll keep the acquisition of particularly volatile content in mind as we move through the chapter.

A note on file formats

Along with hard drive crashes, the experience of having a file in a particular format that you cannot render or read back is probably one of the most common experiences for many outside the field of digital preservation. It is one of the more relatable anecdotes we have about the risks accompanying digital data. Perhaps an older WordPerfect file is incompatible with a user's Microsoft Office suite. Once-prominent multimedia files and web players like the RealPlayer product line have now been discontinued, leaving such files scattered on older sites and drives.

Within the field, this problem is typically referred to as 'file format obsolescence'. We take obsolescence here to describe 'a state of becoming obsolete, rather than already being obsolete', with obsolete being the point at which a file can no longer be rendered, and obsolescent the condition of being likely to be unrenderable in some near time frame (Pearson and Webb, 2008). Discussions usually centre on how to mitigate the risks of obsolescence and prevent any obsolete files from occurring in a collection. The two most used strategies here are format migration – moving the original file format to a new format – and emulation – making software that is compatible with the file (be that a reader or an entire operating system) available to a user, typically through a virtual machine.

We will cover both of these strategies in Chapter 6, but for now let's dig into the problem of format obsolescence a little more. Because of the familiarity many users will have with file format incompatibilities, the risk that obsolescence poses to digital preservation practices can be overstated. Even in the case of an older document incompatible with a newer reader, the file is not obsolete – it can be rendered in the original software in which it was produced. In many cases, a community exists that can assist in moving that older document into a newer version. Barring that, there is often open source software, such as LibreOffice or OpenOffice for office documents, that will probably be able to render back that file as well. Cases of absolutely obsolete file formats are, we suspect, very rare; and would be even rarer for formats introduced after widespread adoption of the internet, as researcher David Rosenthal highlights in his recap of a 2009 Coalition for Network Information (CNI) plenary (Rosenthal, 2009). It is certainly possible to acquire a collection with a significant amount of files featuring formats that are inscrutable or very old (or both, we suspected), but such collections are exceptions; more frequent are the acquisitions of anticipated formats and documents, from office files and common image, audio and video formats, to web documents and components.

It is best to consider your file format strategy in this context. Given the infrequent cases of obsolete or obsolescent formats, it may not be prudent to expend a great deal of time or resources in pre-emptively copying formats to other formats. Those targeted formats may be newer versions of the original's format, or a non-proprietary or open source format. Regardless, unless the user has indicated that they need these particular formats, it is arguable that creating copies for such formats is an unnecessary step. We should also bear in mind that it is best practice to retain the original file format irrespective of which new format you elect to migrate to. Given that practice, there is no particular window of opportunity to target for creating preservation or access copies. In other words, you may be able to wait until there is a demonstrated need for a new format before electing to create that copy.

One aspect of addressing file format obsolescence is file format identification. There are a number of tools available that are designed specifically to investigate files and assign a known format to them. Aside from potentially identifying problematic file formats, these tools can be useful simply to keep a running inventory of what sorts of files are in your repository. Processing software suites such as an Archivematica and BitCurator package use command line format identification tools as part of the automated descriptive process.

Some tools contain their own ruleset for identification, such as JHOVE and the Unix `file` command, while others reference the external PRONOM file format database, run by The National Archives of the UK. Instances of the latter include DROID, Fido and Siegfried, all managed by the Open Preservation Foundation. Each of these tools presents a different set of strengths and weaknesses, so we encourage you to experiment with them (they are all free) to identify which will best suit your needs. Harvard University also maintains FITS, the File Information Tool Set, which attempts to run several file identification tools in a single execution, compiling the resulting information into a comprehensive XML file. Tools wrapped in FITS include DROID and JHOVE, along with other identification or characterisation utilities like ExifTool and Apache Tika.

The PRONOM database is a voluminous resource which can give you an immense amount of detailed information on a large number of file formats. The Library of Congress also maintains a file format information site focused on preservation formats for different types of digital media. We recommend bookmarking their 'Sustainability of Digital Formats' site, as you may end up referencing it frequently to understand potential preservation formats for collection materials in your care.

Thinking about storage

Most computer users are familiar with storage – specifically, the experience of not having enough, or the anxiety of soon not having enough.

Is there space on your smartphone for a new podcast, video recording, set of pictures or application? Is there capacity on your computer for similar types of new content? This day-to-day familiarity allows us to immediately 'get' that there will be no preservation of any digital content if the storage space for it is not there. Yet the raw capacity of storage space is the beginning of our considerations for preservation, not the end. In order to really consider how to actively preserve digital content, we need a new term for long-term retention. Let's call this term 'preservation storage', several steps beyond our personal and daily storage concerns.

Preservation storage

If storage were a perfect technology, it would be easy enough to store our preserved content and leave it be. Of course, you may have had the experience of a hard drive failure or an unreadable USB stick – or you may have heard of someone else's illegible backup drive, or a cloud storage spot going dark. We know then that storage is not a perfect technology or practice. The ways a storage technology or service can go awry are in fact numerous, and range from hardware or media problems to human error, software bugs and financial troubles (Rosenthal et al., 2005). If we are serious about preserving digital content for the long term, we must put in place some strategies to protect from these threats. Let's cover the primary ways to do this.

Replication

Replication is the act of copying your preserved content to multiple storage locations. There are of course a wide array of strategies to do this. Specific strategies for replication of digital content constitute a unique decision for any individual institution, since no private, national or international policy directly specifies the geographic distances and number of copies of a preserved package.

Nevertheless, we have a good deal of guidance on the subject. A 2012 poll of members of the National Digital Stewardship Alliance (NDSA) found a majority of the members keeping all or some of their master copies in multiple geographic locations (Bailey, 2012). The NDSA itself also recommends at least three copies in geographic locations with different disaster threats at the top end of replication performance in its Levels of Digital Preservation chart (see the further reading section for more on this resource). While we will touch on repository certification further down, the *Trustworthy Digital Repositories: attributes and responsibilities*, a Research Libraries Group and OCLC report (2002), also advises at least one geographically remote backup in its Appendix on Archival Storage.

Putting aside the particular advice of these organizations and reports, let's review our top concerns here. Adequate geographic distribution is key to protecting the data from natural disasters, regional blackouts and brownouts or other large-scale disruptions. Sufficiently multiple copies are a catch-all safeguard against software vulnerabilities, human operator errors, media and hardware failures and network transfer failures.

Finally, it is best to strive for at least roughly synchronous copies. By 'synchronous' we mean that changes to one copy of a preserved package are replicated to the other copies of the package in a timely manner. Imagine the overhead costs if you were to adjust the contents or metadata of a preservation package, but those revisions were not communicated down the line to your other copies. We can easily picture such a scenario becoming untenable in short time. It is therefore important to strive for synchronicity in your replication strategy.

Fixity checks and auditing

One of the most relied-upon aspects of computers is their ability to re-present information to us in the exact manner that we left it. If we open a Microsoft Word document, we don't blink an eye when every letter, blank space and even the cursor itself is back to precisely where we left it, even though that document may not have been (virtually) touched or thought of in months or years. If we save a spot in a computer game, there isn't the least thought that reloading that saved game will put us anywhere but in the exact place we left our play. Our smartphone often loads an application back to the specific view we had of it when we left it to take a call, text a friend or leave it for another application.

Yet this seemingly perfect process is in fact the result of many error correction steps along the way, and sometimes these steps do not ensure perfect data replication (Kirschenbaum, 2008, 91). Errors can occur at a number of levels, from bugs in software that produce undocumented changes in a file or its metadata, to file systems that are not always able to rollback incomplete changes when a computer unexpectedly shuts down due to a system freeze or blackout. Even barring these events, the subatomic environment wherein modern transistors conduct their operations is not stable enough to ensure perfectly predictable behaviour. Indeed, high-energy neutrons in the environment can pass through physical casings and silicon boards to actually collide with the microelectronic circuitry of a computer (Cooper, 2012), producing errors ranging from those that are benign, unnoticed and quickly corrected by a system's processes, to those that are not detected and instead settle in as a permanent malfunction in the system, potentially producing errors in cascade.

Given that even perfectly engineered operations will produce errors in time, reliance on checksums has become a standard practice in digital preservation. The checksums we generate when ingesting content into our storage or repository systems are the virtual fingerprints we check back upon in a fixity or integrity check. If you are not familiar with checksums or need a refresher, refer back to our introduction to the subject in Chapter 3. The process is straightforward: the software running the check has a record of the alphanumeric value constituting a file's checksum; the file's checksum is then recalculated to ensure that it matches the record on hand, confirming the file's integrity.

Once again, there is no standard prescribing the precise rates of fixity checks, or even the hashing algorithm best used. On the former subject, we can reference the *Trustworthy Repositories Audit and Certification: Criteria & Checklist* (TRAC), by the OCLC and the Center for Research Libraries (CRL), which recommends fixity checks in criterion B4.4, though no checking frequency is recommended (CRL, n.d.). In general, you should aim to be able to run fixity checks at any time you desire, while also automating that process at a rate which accounts for the processing costs of regenerating all those checksums. It is not tenable to run fixity checks constantly, so monthly, bi-monthly, quarterly or yearly rates can be used instead. On the latter subject, one should generally elect to use more recent and revised hashing algorithms, though this does come at a cost of calculation time.

Long-lived media

We've listed replication, fixity and auditing as key features of a preservation storage strategy. You may notice that we have not mentioned the specific storage devices used. Whether we are opting for spinning-disk hard drives, solid state drives, tape storage libraries, or some combination thereof, we expect routine replacement of the devices as they age or lose their cost efficiency. In all cases, consumer- or enterprise-level brands suffice.

There is often research in 'long-lived' digital media such as quartz or stone DVDs, or even fused silica glass. These developments are fascinating, but it is vital to remember that any given new technology must achieve immense scale to become tenable for long-term storage adoption. There must be a reasonable expectation as well that the software and hardware needed to read data from these devices will be available in the future, or that the data can be generally moved from these new technologies to other storage devices as needed. To our knowledge, highly novel, 'durable' storage devices do not ensure this. As we mentioned earlier in this chapter, managed storage is integral to preservation storage, and prospective long-lived media devices with little or no demonstrated scale or surrounding support communities are going to be very difficult to manage.

Budgeting

> The fundamental problem is not storing bits safely for the long term, it is paying to store bits safely for the long term.
>
> (David Rosenthal, The Medium-term Prospects for Long-term Storage Systems, 2016)

Ongoing funding of digital preservation efforts can be a difficult subject to address. Year-after-year funding of preservation storage systems is often out of the control of an individual archivist or librarian. At an organizational level, this type of routine, long-term planning and funding can be elusive as well. Outside of these considerable challenges, the actual costs of long-term preservation are hard to accurately predict. Yet the economic necessities of digital preservation are probably one of the greatest risks that the effort faces. Consideration of this risk is therefore vital to an inclusive look at born-digital media in archives. One strategy for conceiving of long-term budgets for preservation may be a simple division of costs between (a) the purchase of storage space or devices and the cost of moving data into the system and (b) the ongoing maintenance, service or labour costs of the purchased storage and the cost of moving data out of the system. We will look at both of these areas in more detail.

The purchase of storage is generally an immediate cost that is easier to anticipate in the short term. If you are running a preservation system yourself, the cost of the media and time to install can be estimated. If you are renting storage under a cloud service or other vendor, the vendor's rates are usually posted and known. In either case, however, the cost may change over time. It is important to note here that while the general experience of the individual consumer is of decreasing costs for storage, it is imperative not to rely on overly sunny projections of storage costs. The storage industry is subject to a great deal of change. Events such as the Thailand floods in 2011, which knocked out arms of production for both Seagate and Western Digital, have proven to have long-lasting ripple effects on storage costs, with costs remaining above projected points for two to three years following the disaster (Muncaster, 2012). We also know that there is a limit to the density of information that any media device can hold without corresponding instability in the information bits, requiring further costs to control (if possible) that instability. In other words, it is unreasonable to expect data storage costs to tumble down indefinitely – estimates of future storage costs should be conservative. This allows you to accommodate rises in a vendor's rates, increases in storage device costs and so on.

Moving data into a system also costs in terms of time and labour. In the case of storage vendors, be aware of any hard limits on the amount of data that can be ingested in a given time period – if any exist. Understand as well the amount of time that is estimated to move data into the system, and any labour costs (e.g. any work hours needed to ensure content is ingested) too.

The ongoing costs of maintaining the storage you are using are of course essential. In the case of storage vendors, the annual rates are typically posted. Be aware of course that those rates are typically subject to change. If you or your institution are running a preservation system instead (or as part of a larger solution), the cost of ongoing storage can change as well, though you may be able to better anticipate those changes. In both cases, storage maintenance is connected to an extensive network of surrounding markets and technologies: energy and cooling costs, facility expenses, media replacement, storage software updates, remuneration for technical administrators and so on. While an archive is not typically tracking all these industries and trends, fluctuations in them are communicated down to your storage costs. Remember again that preservation storage is managed storage, and that good, routine management is a substantial cost.

Finally, be mindful of what it costs to take data out of the system. This applies in two scenarios: first, the routine retrieval of the data for researchers, end-users and internal use; and second, the necessity of moving all data out of the system in an effort to relocate the content to a new system or institution. In the first scenario, storage vendors may charge to extract data from their stores after a certain monthly or yearly quota, and that cost may impact on what you allow to go into the system. It is important to note here whether the quota relates to the number of bytes requested or the number of files requested, or whether the vendor maintains limit quotas for both of these tallies. While it is not always the case, born-digital materials often ratchet up the file count faster than digitised material, which tends to have a larger byte-per-file ratio. In the second scenario, if you cannot reasonably reacquire data you have invested into a system *en masse*, you may want to strongly reconsider using that system in the first place. If your strategy cannot ensure that the stewarded content can be moved to a new system or organization, you have introduced a very real risk to the content.

Communicating the need for preservation

All of this may sound overwhelming. Remember, however, that preservation is an ongoing process and taking a first step – even a partial step – is far preferable than no movement at all. One of the most comprehensive studies of the economic challenges of digital preservation was *Sustainable Economics for a Digital Planet: ensuring long-term access to digital information*, a 2010 report by a Blue Ribbon Task Force. There is much to glean from this report and it is well worth a complete read, but we highlight it here because it provides an excellent overview for framing the economic challenges of digital preservation to a wider community.

The report is particularly incisive in characterising digital preservation as a product, similar or dissimilar to other products in a market. As a product, digital preservation holds a status as a derived demand, meaning that users are not interested in preservation *per se*, but in what preservation allows – general access, research, re-use and other affordances. This highlights a possible pitfall in advocating for digital preservation. As enthusiasts and professionals in the field who are deeply involved in the work of digital preservation, we can lose sight of the fact that other parties are interested in digital preservation only insofar as it opens the door to all those uses.

The report also observes that, as a product, digital preservation is a 'nonrival' good, meaning that users may reap the benefits of a preserved digital asset at no cost to any other user. Many other nonrival goods exist as well – a movie, a particular design or a patented algorithm are all examples. When you sit down to watch a movie in a cinema, your 'use' or viewing of the movie doesn't deplete anyone else's viewing. For digital preservation, this non-rival status creates immense potential value to everyone over time, but also opens the door to a 'free rider' problem. Many will benefit from what is preserved and made available, but it is not likely that many will be paying for it. It is likely instead that only a few parties will actually support the costs of preserving digital resources over time. This again highlights an important component of advocacy – funders of digital preservation need to be on board with the wider mission, and may need incentives – such as public recognition – to be attracted to the proposition. We recommend investigating the Blue Ribbon Task Force report for further pointers on how to communicate both the value of digital preservation and the challenges therein to potential stakeholders, funders and users.

Certification

Development of certification and risk assessment programmes has run right alongside the general maturation of the digital preservation field. In this section we will take a look at some of the prominent certifications available now, as well as any prominent antecedents. One of the primary documents in this area is the Open Archival Information System (OAIS), which models how a digital repository functions to preserve data and make it available. This model attempts to be fairly inclusive of all aspects of this work and includes subjects from technical, preservation and descriptive metadata, to storage strategy, ingest process, administration and dissemination of data to users. The model was developed by the Consultative Committee for Space Data Systems, a group designed to create standards and guides for space agencies (see Figure 5.1). Their recommendation was developed into ISO 14721:2003, which was later revised to ISO 14721:2012, and has found significant purchase with the wider archives communities.

One of the most widespread outputs of the OAIS model has been the distinction between data submitted to a repository (the Submission Information Package), the data as held by the repository after processing (the Archival Information Package) and the data as presented to the user (the Dissemination Information Package). These are initialised as SIPs,

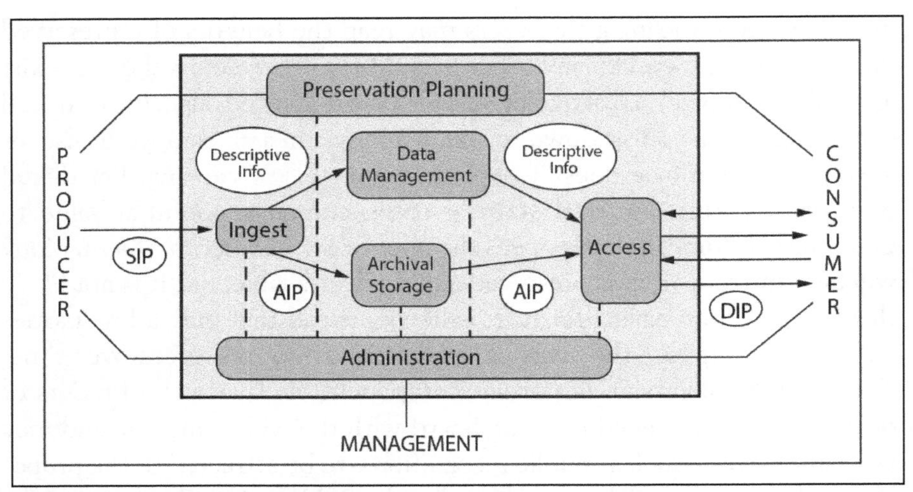

Figure 5.1 *Overview diagram of the OAIS model © NASA, Consultative Committee for Space Data Systems*

AIPs and DIPs, and pronounced 'sips, apes and dips' (for what is a field without its jargon?). In some cases the three versions may be nearly identical, such as a simple text file which only needs some descriptive and technical metadata associated with it, as an AIP. In other cases the versions may alter widely, undergoing processing to a non-proprietary file format, rearrangement or even multiple DIPs to deliver to different communities (DIPs could also incorporate multiple AIPs or parts of multiple AIPs). Other terms found in OAIS are in wide use within the digital preservation field, such as Designated Community, which describes the group(s) to which digital objects are to be made available and legible, along with breaking out an object's metadata into categories such as provenance, fixity, technical and so on.

We won't take a deep dive into OAIS, but there are numerous resources that summarise and review that document – and we'll highlight one in the further reading section. We believe it is important to become familiar with the document and we encourage you to do so. Just note here, however, that the OAIS model is a general framework describing the functions of an archive – it does not produce specific recommendations for institutions (e.g. what metadata profiles to use, what storage technology to purchase or rent, etc.). It provides instead a shared vocabulary, and a set of shared expectations, for the general operations of a repository. We should note here as well that while OAIS has been a useful and formative standard for the archives community, it is not without critique, development or continual re-evaluation.

Because OAIS attempts a comprehensive overview of a digital repository but does not prescribe particular solutions, it can form a foundation for a certification or assessment project. To this end, the Center for Research Libraries (CRL) helped to create ISO 16363:2013, which describes metrics for what a repository ought to do according to the OAIS framework. Naturally following this is a second standard, ISO 16919:2014, which articulates the requirements for any given body to certify a repository as ISO 16363:2013 compliant.

ISO 16363 was initially known as TRAC before revision into the Trusted Digital Repository (TDR) Checklist, so forgive yourself if you experience name confusion here. Several institutions have gone through this certification and audit process at the time of this writing, which you may find on their sites, and reflections on the process from a few different sources are available online as well. Regardless of whether your institution is aiming to undertake that process, the TDR and OAIS documents can be immensely valuable in evaluating your repository and organization.

A second certification process is CoreTrustSeal, which recently replaced the Data Seal of Approval. This certification has its origins in the Data Archiving and Networked Services institute at the Royal Netherlands Academy of Arts and Sciences, along with support from the Netherlands Organization for Scientific Research. The impulse here is similar to what drove the creation of OAIS – a desire to ensure that archived information can still be searched, recovered and used beyond the near-term future. A first version was established in 2008, and the certification is now reviewed and managed by an international board. The certification has 16 requirements and draws its evaluative criteria from TRAC, Digital Repository Audit Method Based on Risk Assessment (generated by the Digital Curation Centre and the DigitalPreservationEurope group) and guidelines from the nestor co-operative group based in Germany. The assessment manual is available online, so once again this effort provides immense value and guidance even if an institution is not prepared for or interested in formally seeking the certification.

Digital preservation policy

A digital preservation policy is fundamentally a statement of intent and commitment by an organization to ensure the longevity of and access to the digital objects it acquires. However, the policy goes beyond this immediate purpose and articulates why a policy is necessary (notably this often leads into a summary of the challenges to preservation, many of which we've covered here), how it contributes to the mission statement and goals of the institution and what the aims of the policy itself are. We think a digital preservation policy is not a perfunctory statement of intent, but a considered engagement with the core activity of digital preservation which may require a fair amount of organizational introspection to achieve. To this end, we will look at the landscape of digital preservation policies here with an eye toward building your own.

Over the years, and especially from the mid-2000s and on, a range of research libraries, archives and other institutions have made their digital preservation policies publicly available. The Library of Congress's own digital preservation blog shared some of the work in this area in 2013 (Sheldon, 2013), and it should not be difficult to discover other policies posted online. One of the best overviews of the digital preservation policy effort is from Ohio State University Libraries, who recount their own policy-making project (Noonan, 2014). This case study breaks down policy into 12 areas, from the organization's mandate (legal or otherwise) and its preservation objectives to the principles underlying the policy and the criteria for selection and acquisition. As you may surmise from the range described there, a digital preservation policy addresses a fairly large list of work areas, and needs to align with the overall goals of the organization. There are similar taxonomies or analyses of digital preservation policies, though we find that each contains significant overlap with others. You may not settle on the same 12 areas or divisions as this particular case study, but do keep this larger scope in mind when drafting. Consider asking the following.

- *Who* is the policy audience? This may be end-users, administration, your department or all the above.
- *What* is the policy addressing? Here you can define digital preservation and other key terms, while setting your scope appropriately.
- *Why* should your organization undertake this project? Again, this may be mandate, larger organizational mission goals or some other responsibility or ambition.
- *When* do you perform digital preservation? I.e. what materials are appropriate for preservation?

- *How* do you perform digital preservation? This may take into account a definition of preservation levels or what services you can agree to provide over time; you may also consider what persons or roles perform which tasks for digital preservation.

With this initial scope in mind, let's look at a few key additional aspects of policies.

Policies and plans should be separate

There may be a tendency to use the digital preservation policy as an opportunity to dive into the specific actions of born-digital preservation, such as file format migration, storage strategy, access mechanisms and description levels. While it is understandable to desire clarity and specificity in these important decisions, we advise against this approach. The best tools, practices and strategies for specific preservation actions are subject to much more flux than an overarching policy for your organization. You may receive items that require exceptions to the general practice, as well. Most importantly, however, the two efforts are not mutually exclusive. We recommend simply allowing your digital preservation policy to reference particular preservation plans as needed. You may have separate preservation plans for audiovisual, forensic images, digitised materials and so on. This allows you to develop those plans independently but to have them reliably derived from the policy. Where you desire specificity in the preservation policy, refer to results and services that you can ensure, regardless of the tools used to achieve them.

Roles, responsibilities and collaboration

We want to emphasise a collaborative roles and responsibilities component here. It is important to consider who in your organization needs to be involved in order for digital preservation to succeed. As noted in Dartmouth College Library's Digital Preservation Policy:

> the expertise to treat analog materials generally exists within one department; for the majority of the Library's physical collections, that department is Preservation Services. The expertise and actions required to preserve digital content exists across multiple departments, including Preservation Services, Digital Library Technologies Group, College Computing, Cataloging and Metadata, and others. A robust digital

preservation infrastructure will inherently operate within a collaborative and communicative workspace.

Imagine running a comprehensive preservation programme. Will you need support from an IT unit, perhaps in areas of data security or server administration? Buy-in from administrative groups? Research expertise or advocacy from computing centres or groups? As we noted in the section above on budgeting, digital preservation has multiple stakeholders and it is important to identify those stakeholders and collaborators in order to mitigate against bearing the total cost and responsibility of preservation – if it is even possible for your organization alone to enact digital preservation at the needed scale. Further, identifying these collaborators will help you to understand the best way to put together a digital preservation policy, since these groups will be a key audience for the document. Bear in mind also that these departments and units are people too – a simple 'thank you' can go a long way to maintaining good relations with the individuals working next to you! However you choose to communicate it, ensure that collaborators know they are appreciated.

Models

You may find it difficult to simultaneously avoid specific actions and plans, yet also describe your preservation goals in a way that is clear to others. Digital preservation models can help here. A few prominent models are the National Digital Stewardship Alliance's Levels of Digital Preservation, Tessela's Digital Archiving Maturity Model, and the Digital Preservation Capability Maturity Model. We encourage you to employ whichever model(s) strike you as germane, lucid and useful to your cause. A key benefit to using these frameworks is the ability to refer to a comprehensive schema of preservation functionality and to locate your institution within that schema. It can also clarify any aspirational goals or directions that you may include in the digital preservation policy (and yes, we do not feel aspirational statements are out of place in a policy document – quite the opposite!).

Finally, we will leave this section with two pieces of advice. Referencing and even adopting pieces verbatim from other policies is fine, so long as this activity does not preclude actual investigation into your specific context, capabilities and aspirations. As we noted at the top of the section, the best policy generation can be something of an introspective effort, where the organization reflects on its purpose and locates a course of action aligned with its mission. A wholesale duplication of an existing policy will prevent this sort of activity from occurring and is likely to leave vital stakeholders in the dark about your policy. Along these lines, make plans to revisit the policy in some set amount of time. Certain events within an organization can prompt reviews regardless, but it is important to have this plan so as to ensure that the policy is appropriately updated and reconsidered. This latter point is especially true with born-digital materials, as the landscape of potentially collectible material changes often. When it does, be sure that you are tying any new strategies or objectives for born-digital material into the larger goals of your organization.

Conclusion

We have covered a good deal on the subject of preservation, from item level to system level. Some of the main points were the following.

- We discussed how acquisition is often the single greatest step in born-digital materials preservation.
- We characterised file format obsolescence as a risk, albeit a smaller threat than it may initially seem.
- We covered thinking about storage for preservation at a system level rather than at a smaller, per hard drive level, and introduced key concepts in preservation storage: replication, fixity check and auditing.
- Budgeting and how the economics of long-term retention and access factor into the work of preservation was also covered.
- We looked at policy and planning for digital preservation.
- Finally, we noted a few prominent digital preservation models to reference in policy and planning work.

Further reading

We've listed below the major resources mentioned in this chapter, along with a number of online resources that you can dig into to become more comfortable with the areas discussed in this chapter.

Blue Ribbon Task Force (2010) *Sustainable Economics for a Digital Planet: ensuring long-term access to digital information, Final Report*

of the Blue Ribbon Task Force on Sustainable Digital Preservation and Access, http://brtf.sdsc.edu/biblio/BRTF_Final_Report.pdf.
As we noted earlier, this is an excellent examination of the economic challenges that often come with digital preservation. The report has great guidance on framing those challenges to outside parties as well.

Digital Preservation Management: implementing short-term strategies for long-term problems (2003) *OAIS Reference Model Overview*, http://dpworkshop.org/dpm-eng/foundation/oais/index.html.
The whole of this tutorial, supported by funding from the National Endowment for the Humanities, developed by Cornell University and currently maintained by MIT Libraries, is a great learning resource. The section for the OAIS reference model (look in the 'Foundations' section) is a good way to test your knowledge on the document and ensure that you're taking in the core concepts there.

National Digital Stewardship Alliance (2012) *Levels of Preservation*, http://ndsa.org/activities/levels-of-digital-preservation/.
The NDSA, as part of the Library of Congress's larger National Digital Information Infrastructure and Preservation Program, has put together a wonderful delineation of multiple preservation capabilities at an institution. In a 5 x 4 matrix, the document outlays preservation functions for Storage and Geographic Location, File Fixity and Data Integrity, Information Security, Metadata and File Formats.

References

Center for Research Libraries (n.d.) TRAC Metrics, www.crl.edu/archiving-preservation/digital-archives/metrics-assessing-and-certifying/trac.

RLG and OCLC Report, *Trusted Digital Repositories: attributes and responsibilities*, www.oclc.org/content/dam/research/activities/trustedrep/repositories.pdf.

CHAPTER 6

Access

> Technology wants us, but what does it want *for* us? What do we get out of its long journey? (Kevin Kelly, *What Technology Wants*, 2010, 347)

Providing access to born-digital content can be both straightforward and exceedingly complex. For those files that are simple, standalone and in common file formats, providing access can be as simple as double-clicking on the file to open it in a contemporary computer with a standard suite of software installed. This is currently true of standalone PDF, DOCX, PPT, JPG, MP3 and AVI files, but less true of older file types like WordPerfect and Windows Media Audio, as well as complex proprietary formats – for example, older versions of AutoCAD. You will also have special considerations to keep in mind when providing access to e-mail, website and mobile device content.

There are several options for providing access to your born-digital content, each with its own benefits and challenges. You may be considering providing unrestricted online access to your content, some form of restricted online access or on-site-only access; you may want to provide a combination of these methods. In this chapter, we'll take a look at some of the options that are available to you for online, remote and restricted on-site access and review some of the additional things you will need to consider for providing access to born-digital content generally.

Deciding on your access strategy

There are several things that you will need to consider when developing your access strategy. First, you will need to have an understanding of the nature of your current and future born-digital content with regard to: the format-specific hardware and software needed in order to provide access; access restrictions imposed by law or donor agreements; and the significant properties inherent to the content that you may or may not need to preserve. Second, you will need to understand your current technological infrastructure and what it can and can't support, as well as have a roadmap for expanding and adapting this infrastructure as your needs grow and the technological landscape changes. Last, it is very important to know your users' requirements for accessing your content.

Nature of your content

The nature of your born-digital content will dictate many of the decisions you will need to make about your access strategy. As noted earlier, simple and ubiquitous file types will not impose access requirements that are overly difficult to meet, but more complex and uncommon types of content may put your institution's ability to provide meaningful access to the test. Additionally, your content may contain elements to which national or regional laws prevent access, or inhibit your ability to provide access, such as PII and copyrights. You will also have to contend with technological restrictions inherent to the content, such as embedded digital rights management (DRM) mechanisms, passwords, encryption and watermarking.

Hardware and software needs

One of the most fundamental aspects of the nature of your content is how it was created and, consequently, what hardware and software is necessary to render its content in a way that is meaningful and useful to the people and machines accessing it. As noted, this is a simple matter for digital content that exists in a current and ubiquitous format. It is not so simple for rare and obscure formats, and over the long term even the most common formats may become increasingly difficult to render.

So, how do you address the hardware and software needs for providing access to your born-digital content now, and how do you plan for technological changes in the future? For more contemporary content, it may be as simple as providing some sort of portal for users to download the content, which they can then easily render on their own computers using common software. For the more challenging formats, there are a growing number of resources available online that you can use to help you determine what hardware and software you and your users will need to render your content (see Appendix A).

Another good option is to make use of the growing community of people who have had or are having similar challenges to yours. You can reach out to informal groups, post questions on listservs or connect with communities focused on solving problems like this such as those involved with the International Conference on Digital Preservation, the NDSA, the Open Preservation Foundation (OPF), the IIPC, the Digital Curation Centre and the Software Preservation Network. If you feel daring, you might also consider reaching out to software developers or even hacker communities who are informally or formally involved in digital preservation activities.

You can also look into software and hardware registries that were created to collect and share data about file formats, software and hardware that you will need to know in order to render your content. For example, PRONOM, hosted by the UK National Archives, is a technical registry that contains information about digital file formats and associated software. You might also take a look at the 'Let's Solve the File Format Problem' wiki, which is a quasi-open wiki that contains similar information on digital file and other information formats.

One of the most challenging aspects of developing processes of providing access to your born-digital content is that of ensuring that the appropriate hardware and software are available to enable you to do so. After accomplishing these challenging yet basic steps, there are additional considerations to keep in mind. Taking into account the general nature of your content, your users' needs and your technological infrastructure, you will also need to think about overall strategies for maintaining your and your users' abilities to render the content over time. As technology advances at an almost exponential rate, it's clear that support for older digital formats will be diminishing in its wake. Currently, there are four strategies to address this growing challenge. You can:

1 maintain hardware and software that is original to the creation of the digital content;
2 create and maintain emulated environments that can host the software needed to render the digital content;
3 establish pathways to migrate the content from an older file format to a currently supported format; or
4 create a strategy that uses a combination of approaches.

You may choose to adopt only one of the first three approaches, or you may adopt a combination of two or possibly all three. There are pros and cons for each of these approaches that you should think about when deciding on your strategy.

The first approach, that of maintaining the original hardware and software used to create and render digital content, can be ideal because it maintains the most authentic rendering environment for the content. With this method, you can provide the best contextual and historical environment for collections. This could be a good solution if your collections are of deep historical importance, and allowing users to experience the environment in which they were created will substantially enhance their interpretation of the content. The downfall of this approach is that it requires a high level of technological competence to maintain the original hardware and software. Other drawbacks are that is is location-constrained access and a pretty high maintenance premium for the institution. Infrequent uses of a resource make managing it routinely even harder. Even then, over time the hardware may fail beyond a reasonable ability to repair it. While this method provides the most authentic access environment, it may be difficult or impossible to sustain over the long term.

If you need to create an authentic environment to access your content, but don't want to maintain the original hardware and software, you can also consider hosting an emulation of the original environment on contemporary hardware and software frameworks. Emory University's Manuscript, Archives, and Rare Book Library in the USA notably created an emulated environment of author Salman Rushdie's Macintosh computers on contemporary computers. As a result, users are able to open platforms that run the old Macintosh computing environments as Salman Rushdie experienced them when he was working during the 1980s and 1990s. The challenge in this approach is that once you create or begin hosting an emulated environment, you are left with a problem similar to the one you would have if you were maintaining the original hardware and software: you will now have to maintain the hardware and software that you used to create the emulated environment. In this case, a second challenge is that the emulation stack is available only in the Emory reading room – not online. Archivists at Emory note that use of this resource is very rare. Choosing this method requires you to commit either to maintaining the emulated environment as you created it or to migrating the content to newly created emulated environments as support for each environment fails over time.

The third approach involves migrating the content from the original file format to a current, supported file format. This can be done either upon acquisition, a process called normalisation; or as the file format becomes more difficult and costly to render, or in common parlance, when the file format approaches obsolescence. This method is beneficial in that it does not require you to maintain aging hardware and software, but this comes at the cost of losing some of the authenticity of the rendering environment. If your institution and your users are primarily interested in the content and have little to no need for additional contextual information, then this method could well serve your needs.

The fourth approach is one in which you have a variety of types of content, a variety of user needs and/or a variety of technological capabilities. It is perfectly reasonable to take a combined approach to maintaining your institution's and your users' ability to render your born-digital content. You may decide to normalise all text documents into PDF files on ingest, to create an emulated environment for a collection of 1990s websites and to maintain on-site cathode ray tube televisions to display 1980s video art. Ultimately, these decisions all depend on your user requirements and your technological infrastructure, which we discuss in more detail below.

Legal restrictions

While one of the largest goals of the library and archives professions is to provide open access to information, there are a number of national and regional laws that prevent this – laws related to copyrights and the privacy of health information, school records and general personal information. It is imperative that you take the time to become familiar with the laws in your country and region that affect the ways in which you may provide access to various types of content. In particular, there are laws in several countries that govern the privacy of certain types of information.

Personal information includes PII like identification numbers, addresses, birth dates, phone numbers and e-mail addresses. There are laws that also apply to the publication or release of health information and school records.

Because of the potential volume of born-digital collection content, the task of locating and repressing or redacting legally private information can seem daunting. Fortunately, there are a number of tools available that partially automate this process. Most of these tools use functions that originate from regular expressions or 'regex'. A regex is a string of characters that comprises a search pattern. These search patterns can be defined to search for types of PII within digital files. For example, the following regular expression from the book *Mastering Regular Expressions*, listed in the further reading section below, can be used to search for an e-mail address:

```
                    \w[-.\w]* ← username
                             \@
[-a-z0-9]+(\.[-a-z0-9]+)*\.(com|edu|info)← hostname
```

The `\w` in the username string indicates that the string should start with a character, the `[-.\w]` allows for full stops and dashes and the * is a wildcard that means 'match anything'. In the hostname `[-a-z0-9]` searches for strings that include letters and numbers, `(\.[-a-z0-9]+)*` begins a search for a similar string that appears after a full stop and `\.(com|edu|info)` begins a search for exact strings matching com, edu or info appearing after a full stop.

This simple regular expression string may look confusing or intimidating, but with a little time and concentration, it isn't all that difficult to decode. Take a minute to examine the string above and see if you can pick out the hints of an e-mail address in the structure. If you can't see it, don't worry; almost all of the regular expressions that you will need to use on your born-digital collections are already programmed into available tools. At the moment, you can find pertinent regex strings embedded in the Bulk Extractor tool that comes bundled with the BitCurator software environment, Columbia University's CUSpider and Stanford University's ePADD e-mail management software, among several others.

In addition to locating and redacting PII, you must also be aware of and address any copyright restrictions that exist on your content. For the most part, copyright operates the same for born-digital content as it does for any other type of content. Unsurprisingly, born-digital content poses some new challenges beyond typical considerations. These challenges show up when dealing with the typically higher volume of born-digital content, and especially in the complex form in which born-digital content can be acquired. In an archival environment, even if the donor signs over all copyright to the content they created, donated content that is acquired on hard drives can contain any number of files created by people other than the donor. Acquisitions of e-mail collections pose similar problems, both in volume and in the prevalence of content written by and otherwise created by people other than the donor.

As noted in Chapter 3, another thing to keep in mind when acquiring born-digital content in the form of whole computers or hard drives is the presence of hidden files. If you have a collection that contains hidden files, you will have to make decisions about if and how you would like to provide access to this content. It's possible that most hidden files will not provide much research value, but there may be some cases, such as certain files found in a drive's trash or recycle bin, that can provide valuable insights for researchers.

To provide certain levels of access, especially for digital content, you either have to own the copyrights to the material or possess a licence from the copyright owner to provide online access. If you neither own the copyrights nor have a licence to provide online access, you will be severely limited in your methods of providing access to your content. Your only options will be to provide on-site access via a non-networked computer, or to preserve the content in a dark archive until the content passes out of copyright ownership.

Technological restrictions

As you are planning for providing access to your content, you may discover that there are also a number of technological restrictions that hamper or prevent your ability to do so. The most common of these restrictions are DRM or intellectual property management (IPM) technologies, encryption, password protection and watermarking.

DRM/IPM technologies are designed to prevent unauthorised copying of intellectual content created and owned by certain entities. The intent of these mechanisms is to protect the creator and intellectual property owner's rights to earn revenue from their property. These types of mechanisms clearly cause problems for those of us whose purpose it is to provide broad access to the intellectual creations and knowledge of the world. What is one to do?

Fortunately, the USA's Digital Millennium Copyright Act, the UK and the European Union's Copyright Directive and the French Loi sur le Droit d'Auteur et les Droits Voisins dans la Société de l'Information (DADVSI), while largely designed to protect copyright owners, do include some legislation that allows libraries and other cultural heritage institutions the right to make and distribute copies of certain digital content for noncommercial purposes. Circumventing DRM/IPM technologies does involve having to seek out and employ decryption tools that are largely considered to be illegal. However, there are many such tools that are widely available, and, as with managing hardware and software needs for rendering your born-digital files, the best approach for finding the best circumvention software to date will be to reach out to your community of fellow born-digital content managers.

Encryption is somewhat of a double-edged sword for managing digital content in libraries and archives in that it allows us to protect private and sensitive information, but if the data is encrypted and you don't have the key to decrypt it, it is effectively inaccessible. Your first defence against encrypted files preventing your ability to provide access to your content is to make sure that you have the key to decrypt any encrypted files that you acquire. If you do end up with encrypted files for which you have no key and do not have any means of acquiring one, your only option is to hack the encryption yourself (very unlikely to be successful) or wait for quantum computing to be developed enough to make current encryption standards obsolete (also an unsuccessful strategy). The moral of the story here is that encryption can be an insurmountable barrier to access, surmountable only by planning ahead and ensuring that any encrypted content you acquire comes with a working decryption key.

Similarly to the function of encryption, password-protected files promise to prevent access to the content of the file unless you or your users have the password to unlock the file. When acquiring born-digital content it is imperative that you ask the donor if they know of any password-protected files within the acquisition. It is possible that the donor is unaware of existing protected files in the collection, in which case you are left with the same improbable options that you have with encrypted files; the results of which are inaccessible files.

The last technological restriction that we discuss here is digital watermarking, which is some sort of mark or signal inserted into a digital image, audio file or video file that indicates copyright ownership of the content. While this practice may not restrict wholesale access to the content, it may present unwanted hampering of clear interpretation and use of the content. If, in the process of acquiring born-digital content, you are also acquiring the copyright ownership of the content, you should request that any watermarking be removed from the content before it is transferred to your institution.

User requirements

Understanding the nature of your content isn't enough to design a well thought-out access strategy. You should also take some time to learn about the types of people who will want to access the content. Taking a user-centred design approach to devising access procedures and systems will ensure that you will be able to provide the best access to the greatest number of users. This approach involves several steps.

The first is to actively learn about the people who currently and who may in the future access your content. Second, and most important, you need to collect from various stakeholders the requirements they have for working with your access systems and procedures and for accessing and using your content. In this phase you will need to engage with your stakeholders and ask them about their needs and requirements. You can then use the list of collected requirements to help you determine the functional requirements of your system.

It's also a good idea to draw up sketches or personas of at least three types of people who will access your collections. Flesh out as many details about these people as you can, including name, age, location, occupation, hobbies and any anticipated needs or frustrations they may have in accessing your collections. Using these profiles, you can build various scenarios where these personas may be attempting to access and use your content. For example, if we have a persona of a 24-year-old higher education student who is conducting research on digital video art methodologies over time, you can think about what type of content this person may want to access, how they may want to access it and how they may want to use it in their research. Imagining scenarios like this will help you to discover novel ways of providing access, as well as any issues you need to address along the way.

Significant properties

While discussing or researching the topic of digital collections, you may have come across the phrase 'significant properties'. In this context, significant properties are those properties of a digital object that are important to the interpretation of its content. This has also been described by the phrase 'significant characteristics' or as the 'essence' of a digital object. Significant properties you will need to consider are the content itself, its context, look and feel, functionality and structure. The extent to which you preserve and provide access to each of these significant properties will be determined by mission, mandates and your user requirements. You should ask yourself the following questions.

- Is the mission of my institution or department to preserve all aspects of our collections, some aspects, or are we primarily concerned with the content?
- Are we mandated by higher authorities such as our national or regional government, or other governing agencies, to preserve and provide access to just the content of our collections, or must we also preserve and provide access to other significant properties that support the determination of authenticity?
- Do those seeking to access and use our collections require the look and feel, functionality, context and structure of the digital object(s) in order to understand and interpret its significance for their research?

These are just a few questions you can ask yourself when making decisions about how to present your collection material to your users. The answer to these questions will guide how you shape your access procedures and determine your technological needs to make procedures possible.

Accessibility

Another thing that you will need to consider when designing access systems is their accessibility to people who have disabilities or special needs. Take some time to think about how people with mobility, communication, hearing and visual impairments will access your content. Also think about how people who are colour-blind, who experience seizures or who have cognitive or intellectual disabilities might experience your access system and your content.

Some institutions have units that review systems for accessibility and can provide an overview of how your system addresses the issue. There are also several other resources that you can use to help you evaluate your access system. There are a number of guidelines to which you can refer for guidance, the most notable of which is the Web Content Accessibility Guidelines 1.0 developed by the World Wide Web Consortium. There are also guidelines for web accessibility that have been developed by authorities in Canada, the Philippines, Spain, Sweden, Japan and the UK. In addition to referencing existing guidelines, you can also use one or more of the tools available online that is designed to test websites for accessibility issues.

It's important to keep this in mind when you are designing your access systems, and it's a good idea to work these considerations into your process of collecting user requirements. To best facilitate usability, you should also plan to invite people with disabilities and who have special needs to participate in usability testing of your systems. Ultimately, it's just common sense that designing for broad accessibility benefits everyone.

Arrangement and presentation

Another thing to keep in mind is how you arrange and present the content you've acquired in a way that either facilitates easier access or preserves the context of how the items relate to each other. The way you choose to arrange your content is usually visible in an archival finding aid, in a navigation page in a CMS or in a card catalogue. Here we will discuss how this work applies to the range of born-digital materials. Perhaps more than any other subject covered, arrangement is a process supporting many diverse solutions, depending on institutional or collection goals. This is true for the presentation of strictly physical materials in a finding aid, and it is certainly true of born-digital materials, which frequently complicate conventional takes on the archival principles of original order and provenance.

Original order

We first talked about original order in the context of the forensic acquisition of born-digital materials – materials acquired on a particular piece of physical media, with a distinct order, from the originator of the content. In cases like these, the preservation of original order is relatively straightforward in concept (if not always in execution!) – we want to preserve the organization that the originator handed to us on the media we received. We also covered cases where this was not applicable, i.e. where the media was simply a transporting unit for the digital content and did not contain traces of the originator's actions or any valuable original order.

Note that when we preserve the original order of a group of files on a media device through forensic imaging, we are capturing both the directory structure and the metadata managed by the file system. Unlike for physical items, however, original order *does not* apply to the sequence of the files in any given directory. That listing can be done alphabetically, by file format, creation date or a number of other criteria, depending on the software used to make the listing. We mention this here to emphasise that when we talk about original order for born-digital materials, we are referring only to the directory structure (if the creator didn't set everything in a single directory!) and potentially the metadata associated with those files.

Original order is less applicable in the case of network-born media, such as websites and social media posts, because they are managed and served up by remote software systems and are not located on any particular machine. In acquiring such media, you will want to capture the necessary organizational structure to render the media back, such as the graphics, stylesheets and constituent pages of a website. Of course, this is less 'original order' than it is simply retaining the structure of the object you want to preserve. Other digital content types do not wholly align with the usual notion of original order. A relational database, for example, contains both the content of the database itself as well as the logical structure that divides and recombines that data as needed. It has no 'original order' beyond the integrity of the relational database itself. In addition, you are often acquiring these materials singly – one at a time. If you were to acquire papers from a university professor physically one at a time over a course of weeks, there would be no original order to manage. The same applies here.

When you are considering how original order should inform the arrangement of digital objects, consider closely the acquisition process and nature of the object itself. Complex digital objects, such as websites and databases, acquired outside the context of the originating body, often do not have any original order to retain – though you will want to document the *context* of these acquisitions to whatever extent you can – the tools used to do so, the date of the action, and other conditions of the process.

Applying (or not) original order to the arrangement

In the cases where you *do* have an original order to consider, born-digital objects present both unique affordances and complexities for arrangement. We suggest a two-part process to help you manage this particular task.

First, ask yourself what original order you aim to preserve. This may be the original directory structure and file listing as it was received on a hard drive or floppy disk. As we described earlier (Chapter 3), you may capture this through a forensic image of the disk or transcribe it in some other manner. Or, original order may be a specific group of CDs found in one case as distinct from another group of media found in a second case.

In either of the above examples, however, we can imagine cases where received order is not of interest. A directory structure may simply reflect which department created which file – an organization that will be reflected in the intellectual arrangement located in the finding aid anyway. Or the creator may have simply placed all their files in their 'desktop' directory – usually manifested as the background of their starting screen. A box of digital media may simply be a container used to move the contents to the institution, or an arbitrary container of several for such media. It is up to the archivist to determine if the original order is of value or not.

Second, ask yourself how you aim to reveal any original order in the finding aid. It can of course easily be the case that the original order, while valuable, is not in itself the most clear and useful way to arrange the material in the finding aid. This is often the case in received physical materials, and it is arguably even more often true in received born-digital materials.

In 2005, the Harry Ransom Center in the USA took in the born-digital writings of author Michael Joyce. In processing these materials they found a valuable original order in the manner Mr Joyce backed up and preserved his working and final copies. However, presenting that original order directly (or exclusively) to the end-user would not be the clearest way to organize the collection. They opted to use a more traditional division of his works (with series such as Works, Correspondence and Personal), concluding that a balance could be struck between retaining some original order of the material while imposing external order to make the content easier to access.

There are a number of strategies for representing the original order in the arrangement presented in the finding aid. You may find that a level of arrangement (e.g. a subseries) will accommodate the original order. For example, within a 'Works' series you may have a subseries of 'Digital works' or 'Electronic drafts' that can list the digital media containing those items. More typically, however, we imagine that digital media and the attendant original order therein will contain items spanning across the series or subseries of your collection. In those cases, there may be methods of attaching their original order to the items themselves, so that researchers are aware of this context. For example, an electronic Microsoft

Word draft may be delivered to the end-user coupled with a directory listing from the digital media on which it was found. Alternatively, you may find a way to provide the disk image itself to the researcher as a means of delivering the requested content – in those cases you are already delivering the original order as part of the access method. Another strategy here may be to simply record the original order in a control or administrative file for the collection, and provide the information or access to this document upon request.

Hybrid collections

Hybrid collections are collections containing both physical and born-digital materials. While we do not have numbers from major libraries and archives around the world, it is reasonable to assume that many, if not most, collections will be of this variety for the foreseeable future. The work outputs of professionals – from artists to intellectuals to researchers and organizational leaders – will include both physical and computer-based material.

This is also true of organizational records. Libraries may acquire or purchase materials that are entirely born digital, such as business data, satellite images of Earth terrain or just electronic journals, but even in these cases those materials must often be tied to previous physical materials in the same domain.

The typical goal in hybrid collections is to present a seamless search and arrangement across the realms of the physical and digital. In other words, the user or researcher should not have to consider whether the desired material is physical or digital; they ought only to consider the substance of the material they are looking for and seek it by that criterion. We believe the approach to arrangement described above works very well for hybrid collections with this general goal. It allows the collecting institution both to be attentive to original order and to virtually 'interleave' digital content into a series with other germane physical content in the finding aid itself.

Of course, researchers often *do* look for material by criterion other than by the content itself – they may search by date, for example. In the digital realm, the metadata they may wish to search by are expanded. We can imagine a user looking for all files of a certain format, under or above a certain byte size, within a certain directory or last modified by a certain date. They may simply be interested *only* in those parts of the collection which are born digital. The particular requests of researchers are never entirely predictable, and we will have to rely on both the expertise of collection stewards to accommodate these requests and the increasing sophistication of finding aid software and collection management interfaces.

Third-party materials in arrangement and context

Archives will be familiar with third-party materials in collections. For researcher collections, these are often texts and articles referenced by the donor, or research tools used by them for analysis of collected data. In born-digital acquisitions, the number of third-party materials collected may grow significantly. In a physical donation, a professor will typically leave out student papers they received, but those files may remain on their disks and hard drives. Software applications used for analysis or simple production of work (something as commonplace as Microsoft Word, for example) can be included as well.

Particularly for born-digital acquisitions, third-party materials may constitute a significant portion of the context and original order. It is helpful to understand that a creator used a certain software application to make or edit a file – especially if it is a less common application. The presence and arrangement of other third-party materials often indicates a great deal about how the donor worked, as well.

Ultimately, it will be up to the collecting institution to judge whether these contextual insights are valuable, or if the original order ought to retain third-party materials either in description or in actual retention. Usage rights here will be hugely consequential. It will probably not be possible to present a student paper to a researcher at all, and it may not even be possible to note that the paper was present in the acquisition. Conversely, noting that a directory retained a copy of a piece of software is likely to be admissible, and it may even be possible to provide onsite access to that software under the fair use argument.

Once again, we advise a two-part process. First, determine if the third-party material collected constitutes a critical dimension of the context and original order. If you determine that it does, investigate what options are available for documenting that original order or providing access to those third-party materials.

The arrangement of born-digital materials in a collection should align with the overarching intellectual divisions for that particular collection. We acknowledge that some instances of those intellectual divisions may include a series, subseries or groupings for born-digital materials, but it will more likely be the case that born-digital materials are located within groupings that pertain to aspects other than whether an item is physical or born digital. To that end we have:

- described the characteristics of original order to consider when deciding on retention of this collection aspect;
- described a two-part decision process for integrating original order into your final arrangement;
- considered how hybrid collections align with this strategy; and
- described how third-party materials may contribute to content and original order – and potential strategies for preserving this contribution.

Technological infrastructure

Once you have a clear understanding of the nature of your content, your users' requirements for access and finally your desired arrangement and presentation of your content, you will be able to compare these needs to what your current and planned technological infrastructure can handle. The things you need to know are: your institution's amount of currently available and planned digital storage for access versions of your content; internet data speed; what systems you have available to serve as access portals; and the ability of the system to create various levels of access restrictions.

We discussed storage in Chapter 5, but in addition to needing robust storage for the long-term preservation of your born-digital content, you also need to have a storage system that is capable of providing ready retrieval to access copies of the content. Instead of the content being in what can be called 'deep storage', which requires regular fixity checks and isn't necessarily readily accessible, it should be available in a platform that can serve up the content quickly, securely and accurately.

One of the qualities that differentiate preservation storage from access storage is the speed with which data can be downloaded from the storage platform. Quick download times require fast internet speeds. The size and quality of your storage system in this case can be measured only by how quickly and securely the data can be downloaded. Think of the analogy of a giant lake and a tiny drinking straw, where the lake is the digital object your user wants to access and the straw is the internet connection speed.

In this analogy, you want to be sure that you have something much bigger than a tiny straw for your user to 'download' the lake!

You also need to think about how your users will be able to discover and access your content. Make sure you have useful and easy-to-use access portals. These can take the form of something as simple as a directory on an external or networked drive, or as elaborate as a polished web portal. Whatever the case, be sure to be aware of what your institution currently supports, and think about whether or not you would like to change or improve it.

Beyond providing an access portal, you will probably want to be able to provide different levels of access for different types of system users. You should be able to create different access restrictions for yourself, for advanced tech administrators, data- and content-entry employees, high-level users or basic users. Think about the different types of uses your system should support and be sure that your system can accommodate these different levels.

Methods of access

One of the final steps in providing access to your born-digital content is deciding on the method or methods of serving it up to your users. There are a few approaches you can take to do this: you can deliver your born-digital content online, remotely or on site.

Online access

When most people think of digital content provided by libraries and archives, they imagine being able to access it online. In most cases, this is the ultimate goal, since providing online access to your content will allow for the broadest access to the greatest number of people, which satisfies one of the strongest directives of the library and archives professions, which is to provide open access to as much information to as many people as possible. Providing online access to born-digital content can be as straightforward as providing access to simple digital files such as PDFs and JPGs. However, you may have complex disk images, linked files and difficult-to-render file formats which make providing online access to this content more of a challenge.

Online access platforms

There are quite a few existing platforms for delivering digital content online, ranging from very simple and common systems designed for general content, like WordPress, to complex systems designed specifically for born-digital content, like BitCurator Access. We will explore some of the most common access systems that are currently available, highlighting features you may want to look for in any system when you are designing access protocols and systems at your institution.

- **BitCurator Access**, currently in alpha phase of release, is designed to provide web-based access to content encoded in disk images. It also provides redaction capabilities and emulation services.
- **CONTENTdm** is a digital CMS with a robust discovery interface. The system allows for tiered access restrictions and standards-based description.
- **Drupal** is an open source CMS that can be used for a number of online content hosting scenarios. It is not built with born-digital content in mind, but can be adapted to serve basic content hosting needs. It does provide robust user registration and access hierarchy capabilities.
- **DSpace** is an open source repository package with a focus on long-term storage, access and preservation of digital content.
- **ePADD** was created to process, host and provide access to e-mail collections. It was created specifically for cultural heritage institutions and has many features that serve the needs of e-mail content, such as redaction across complex e-mail collection structures.
- **Islandora** is an open source software framework that combines Fedora, Drupal and Solr technologies to manage and provide access to digital content. This platform was designed with the cultural heritage community in mind and has a number of 'solution packs' to provide domain-specific solutions to its users.
- **Omeka** is an open source web publishing or digital exhibit platform designed for libraries, archives, museums and scholars. Plug-ins are available which provide access restrictions for guest users, and specialised metadata fields.
- **Preservica Universal Access** is a component of the Preservica digital preservation suite that is designed to provide web access to your digital content. The system provides support for born-digital content and allows for internal and public portal access restriction.
- **Samvera** was created as an open source repository application

designed for libraries and archives and is part of the Hydra-in-a-box project. It consequently has capabilities for standards-based metadata, preservation and multilevel access control.
- **WordPress** is an open source CMS. It can allow for hierarchical access restrictions and has numerous plug-ins available that can be used to add needed functionality. This may not be the most robust solution, but the barrier of entry is low enough for small institutions with little funding and small, simple collections to get started.

These are but a sampling of the most common options available. You can explore these options, but also reach out to others in the community for alternatives. You can decide on the best option for you through a thorough analysis of your user requirements and technological infrastructures.

Remote and restricted online access

You may have a situation where you are able to provide access to your content online but need to apply some access restrictions on the content. This may be owing to not owning the copyrights, not having a licence that allows for broad online access, or the existence of sensitive or private information that you either choose not to or are legally prohibited from releasing online. In this case, you may choose to provide remote access to the content, where the user can log in to the system using access credentials that you provide to them. Using this method, you can limit who has access to the content, and possibly limit what content which users can see.

On-site access

Another option to explore is providing content on site. This can entail a number of options ranging from providing the content on non-networked computers with strict security on copying files, to simply providing an access station that connects to your freely available online content. One of your primary concerns in providing on-site access will be selecting the appropriate hardware and all accompanying cables, monitors, headphones or other accessories a user may need to access the content on the machine. You will also have to ensure that the computer you provide for access has the appropriate software installed to render the files you provide.

One other consideration is the level of restrictions you want to place on your access set-up. There are several different approaches that you can take to implementing restrictions on your access computer. You can provide your content via an online network with varying degrees of access restrictions, either by user or by restricting access by IP address. You may also provide the content on a non-networked computer with content served on an external hard drive. To prevent the copying of files you can disable, or have your IT support disable, the USB and other connecting portals on the access machine. Similarly, there is software available that you can use to disable Wi-Fi and Bluetooth connectivity, which will prevent the machine from connecting to the internet and the Bluetooth protocol. If you use this method, you can perform regular software updates by using an ethernet cable or by reactivating Wi-Fi. Remember too, if you have IT support at your institution, that you can do this in co-ordination with them for best results.

Use case

Here we will present you with a hypothetical situation where an archive has received a donation of papers from the famous author, Walker Sampson. Walker began writing stories as a young man using the word processing software WordPerfect on a DOS machine. Amazingly, Walker still had the original computer on which he wrote these stories, and stacks of 5.25" floppy disks that contained his early work; all of which he donated to the archive. In his donor agreement, Walker signed over copyrights of all of his works, except for drafts and manuscripts related to his three most recently published books. In the agreement, he stipulated that the copyright for these items would pass to the archives at the time of his death. In the meantime, the archive is permitted to allow researchers to access the files in question, but they may not be published openly online. These files were provided to the archive in Microsoft Word format on several USB flash drives.

After noting Emory University's struggle with maintaining an on-site, emulated platform for Salman Rushdie's works, and considering the challenge of maintaining a TRS-80 computer over time, the acquisitions archivist decided to politely turn down the offer of the computer, but did excitedly accept the 5.25" floppy disks. The processing archivist then created disk images of the disks, after first taking photographs of the disks and noting relevant metadata written on the disk labels. Since the files of interest from the floppy drives were in WordPerfect format, the archivist decided to separate the files from the disk images for easy access.

The WordPerfect and Microsoft Word files were described and uploaded in the archive's repository system. The WordPerfect files were published openly online. Only the descriptions of the Microsoft Word files were published online, while the files themselves were not and could be accessed only by archive employees who were granted the appropriate access levels to see them. When the archive received requests to view these files, they would invite the researcher into the archive's reading room where access to the files would be provided on a non-networked computer.

Conclusion

Ultimately, the primary purpose of collecting, managing and preserving born-digital content is to provide access to it. This is no simple feat, but not an insurmountable one. Once you have a firm understanding of some of the technological underpinnings of the task, it's only a matter of understanding your users' needs – both internal and external – and your institution's ability to meet them, for you to fulfil this purpose. After reading this chapter, you should have a better sense of:

- How to make decisions about your access strategy based on the nature of your content, technological needs, and your users' requirements.
- Determining how to evaluate and address legal restrictions.
- Approaching technological restrictions like digital rights management and intellectual property management (IPM) technologies, encryption, password protection and watermarking.
- How to arrange and present your born-digital content.
- What types of systems are currently available to assist in providing access to various types of born-digital content.

Further reading

AIMS Workgroup (2012) *AIMS Born-digital Collections: an inter-institutional model for stewardship*, https://dcs.library.virginia.edu/files/2013/02/AIMS_final_text.pdf.

The first and only report of its kind, this white paper is a representation of the efforts of the University of Hull, Stanford University, University of Virginia and Yale University to examine and share current practice for managing born-digital collections. While this paper is useful to review for all aspects of managing born-digital collections, there is particularly good information for providing access.

Carroll, L. L., Farr, E., Hornsby, P. and Ranker, B. (2011) A Comprehensive Approach to Born-digital Archives, *Archivaria*, **72**, 61–92.

This article describes Emory University Manuscripts, Archives, Records, and Book Library's innovative approach to providing an emulated version of Salman Rushdie's old Macintosh computers.

Friedl, J. E. F. (2006) *Mastering Regular Expressions*, O'Reilly Media, Inc.

This is a great, beginning-level book on regular expressions. It begins with the very basics and provides techniques and examples in Java, .NET and PHP.

Guerrero, M. (2012) *Removable Media and the Use of Digital Forensics*, Bentley Historical Library.

An early report on physical media and using digital forensics, sponsored by the Institute of Museum and Library Services.

Hamill, L. (2017) *Archival Arrangement and Description: analog to digital*, Rowman & Littlefield.

This book provides sound guidance on deciding how to arrange your born-digital content.

Kay, G. (2016) *Accessing Born-digital Content: a look at the challenges of born-digital content in our collection*, The National Library of Australia blog, www.nla.gov.au/blogs/preservation/2016/08/09/accessing-born-digital-content.

In this blog post, Gareth Kay describes his experiment in providing access to various born-digital content at the National Library of Australia.

Kiehne, T., Spoliansky, V. and Stollar, C. (2005) *From Floppies to Repository: a transition of bits*, University of Texas at Austin.

This very useful case study walks you through the process of preserving the Michael Joyce digital papers at the Harry Ransom Center at the University of Texas at Austin.

Lowdermilk, T. (2013) *User-centered Design*, O'Reilly Media, Inc.

This is a short, simple resource that clearly describes everything you need to know about using a user-centred design approach.

University of Oxford, University of Manchester (2008) *Paradigm Workbook on Digital Private Papers*, Paradigm Project, www.paradigm.ac.uk/workbook/.

The Paradigm Project produced an online workbook with extensive information about managing digital 'papers'. The entire workbook is a useful reference for managing born-digital content, but, for this chapter, the sections on arrangement and legal issues are particularly relevant.

CHAPTER 7

Designing and implementing workflows

> No, Watson, this was not done by accident, but by design.
>
> (Sir Arthur Conan Doyle, *The Adventures of Sherlock Holmes*)

A series of actions needs to be taken to address the management and access of born-digital materials in an institution – or more precisely, you need to put all of the processes that we have discussed up to this point together somehow. When archivists and librarians discuss that series of actions, they typically refer to it as a workflow. Workflows may address any – and potentially all – aspects of the institution's responsibilities vis-à-vis born-digital collection materials.

The benefits of creating and using workflows are many. Workflows illustrate a unified and principled handling of born-digital materials, and clearly articulate that to staff and trainees. Workflows can also function as a record of what actions the institution performs for its materials. To that end, workflows need not be static references, but living documents; an ongoing project, capable of being amended or adjusted as conditions change.

A note on tools

We find that perhaps the best benefit of workflows is the adjustment in analytical and strategic thinking. Workflows allow you to draw out ideas in a more visual or impromptu manner, and even to incorporate spatial logic into your document (e.g. important steps have larger shapes and more minor steps have smaller outlines) if you care to do so. Even if you do not prefer a visual representation, quickly jotting down your lists and steps is a good break from formal writing. In other words, a key benefit is the opportunity to 'think on paper' in a different way than you might were you to draft a report or policy.

There are many software tools available to create visual workflows, and many of these conform to the Unified Modeling Language (UML). UML is a shared schema of shapes and visual cues to indicate a great deal of the logic you may either find or want to display in a workflow: decision points, relationships and dependencies, among numerous others. While there is certainly a place for this level of formalism and interoperability, we suggest that you disregard it as you begin creating workflows. The best tool will be the one which gets out of your way, and for many that will be paper and pencil or marker and whiteboard. You can always loop back and rework your workflow into a more presentable process document, but don't let yourself get bogged down by software or strict schematics. The primary goal is to think clearly – you don't want to spend that time fighting a tool with which you're unfamiliar.

Design principles

While workflows are a general concept that most practitioners understand easily, we find that workflows themselves very quickly move to the highly specific. This is not to say that there are not commonalities and broad overlaps in workflows, but the bulk of the content of most workflows is institution specific. Nevertheless, we want to provide you with some guiding principles for when you begin designing your own workflows.

Audience

Who are you drafting a workflow for? In many cases, the audience will be either yourself or the individuals performing regular duties in processing and managing born-digital materials. However, you may draft workflows for other audiences, such as people outside of the collecting group. They may be the administrators of your institution, or researchers who are enquiring about your practices. They may also be potential donors who want to understand your practices, or a specific workflow may be *for them*, e.g. how to transfer their materials to your institution. While workflows designed for outside parties are less common, it is worthwhile considering the communicative value of such a document directed to such audiences. Regardless, take note of the audience who will be referencing or seeing this workflow.

Break it down

As we noted at the start of the chapter, workflows can address any or all of the aspects of handling born-digital materials. However, we do not suggest that you attempt a single workflow that covers all such aspects, or even a workflow that covers many of them. We find that such workflows quickly become unwieldy and overwhelming, both for the designer and the user. Instead, consider ways in which you might break down the chain of actions from acquisition to access. For example, you may create a workflow in which you address the immediate inventorying of digital media devices received in a collection. This task would precede any direct work with the contents of that media, but it would cover what descriptive aspects of the media you record. For example, do you record the brand or density type of floppy disks? Do you record whether a CD is a CD-R, a CD-ROM or a CD-RW? How do you document a hard drive – by capacity, brand, physical size (e.g. a 3.5" drive, a 2.5" laptop drive or an external USB-connected drive), recording mechanism (e.g. spinning disk or solid state) and so on? The answers here may be quite straightforward – you may decide that simply counting the quantity of a media type is sufficient – but even smaller tasks have decision points to resolve that you may not consider if your workflow scope is too expansive.

Other workflow segments could include:

- transferring data off a media device
- post-transfer processing of digital content, potentially covering
  - deduplication
  - virus scanning
  - sensitive information scanning
- describing digital content
- ingesting content into your repository system
- integrating digital content into your finding aid.

There will be many ways to construct these divisions, depending upon your particular situation. Regardless, the strategy of breaking down a master workflow into constituent parts will make your task much more approachable and ultimately much more useful.

The input and output pipeline

Particularly when you begin addressing digital content processing, it can be useful to approach your workflow from the standpoint of input-output design. The basic sequence of handling some *input* with a resulting *output* is common in a born-digital workflow. For example, your input may be a file received from a donor. That file receives some processing, after which we have an output, in this case the original file along with an access derivative and a new descriptive document. From this point, you might submit that output as the input for the next step, where you submit the original and access derivative into your repository system.

Under this framework a great deal of the work of born-digital processing and general management can be organized as a series of inputs and outputs, with each output serving as the input for a the next step in the chain. This is a common design pattern in software and computer design, and is also referred to as a pipeline (Figure 7.1).

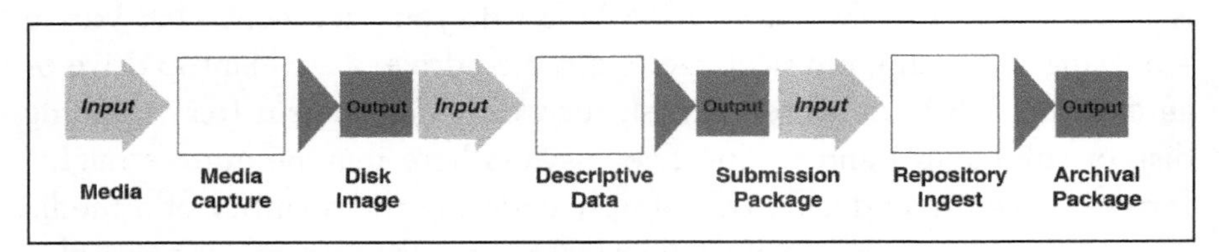

Figure 7.1 *A basic input–output pipeline for a media capture and ingest*

You may consider structuring a workflow – particularly a workflow centred on direct processing of the materials – in this manner. Analyse at each step what the input is, what processes or steps are enacted upon or with that input and what the resulting output will be.

Open source, interoperable, non-proprietary

You may find in the pipeline approach a natural affinity for non-proprietary, open source or widely compatible software and formats. A process that outputs a CSV spreadsheet file will be more interoperable than one that outputs Microsoft's Excel format. As you consider different systems, from processing suites like BitCurator and Archivematica, to repositories and access platforms like Islandora and DSpace, you should be aware of both the characteristics of the software – is it open source, and is there a strong community centred on the software and its use – and the interoperability of its outputs and its general compatibility with other software you may use. You need to avoid deploying tools in your workflow that wrap your content in highly custom formats that are less able to serve as useful inputs for your next step.

In the example in Figure 7.2 opposite, we see how an initial set of disk images receives processing and description while moving through a group

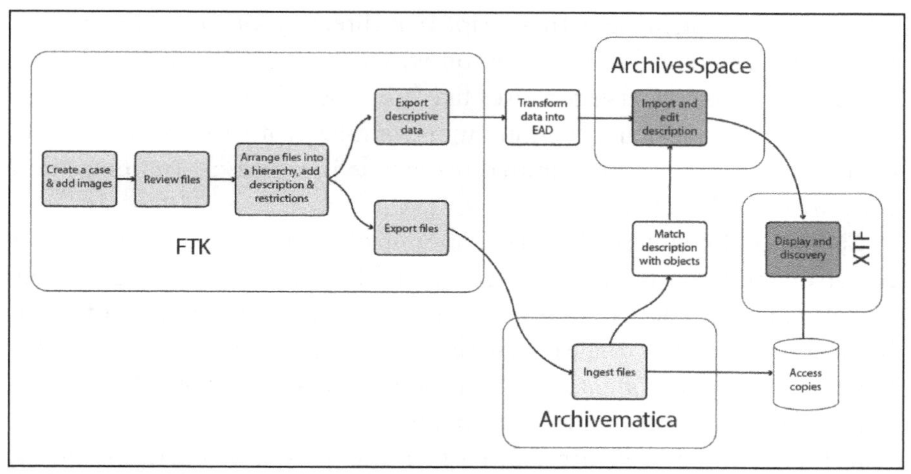

Figure 7.2 *Slide from 'Arrangement and Description for Born Digital Materials', Rockefeller Archive Center © Bonnie Gordon and Hillel Arnold, Rockefeller Archive Center*

of applications. Processing work starts in FTK Imager, a forensic toolkit for Windows. Descriptive data moves into ArchivesSpace, while the files from the disk image are further processed in Archivematica. The workflow also references a process for matching the ingested files to the ArchivesSpace description, and a final output to the institution's access software. This work was presented at CURATECamp 2015 by Bonnie Gordon and Hillel Arnold from the Rockefeller Archive Center, and it contains illustrative workflows for the major steps described here as well, which is a good demonstration of breaking down your workflows into manageable parts (Gordon and Arnold, 2015).

Automation

Closely related to the pipeline design approach is the goal of automation. Once you have described or created a useful pipeline for your digital materials, you will probably begin to consider where in this chain of inputs and outputs you can automate the labour. If it is possible to allow a software process, such as a script, to perform the steps mediating an input and output process, it seems wise to do so.

There are two key variables here. The first is whether the tools you are using in a process are command line operations, or if they are have command line modes. While there are automation frameworks for graphical environments, they are far less interoperable or flexible than what you might achieve with a script that directs your suite of command line tools. This is part of the reason why command line tools are seen frequently in technical enterprises like born-digital content handling, and why you may consider becoming more familiar with the command line environment – there are minimal overheads involved in wrapping these programs into larger workflows.

The second key variable is the amount of decision making needed in any given input–output step. If a considerable amount of evaluation needs to be made, that deliberation raises the cost of automation significantly because you must formalise that process to code it into the computer. Further, some components of a workflow, such as high-level description, may not be amenable at all to automation.

In the example in Figure 7.3, part of a larger entry on automation at *The Signal* (England and Hanson, 2017), both of the CSV steps under the Sampled Directory step are performed by scripts. In both instances, the input is predictable. In the first case, a script takes a directory listing and produces a CSV spreadsheet of those filenames and their metadata. In the second case, a modified CSV is used to adjust directory names. These are both good examples of where automation can be useful: simple, predictable inputs with routine processes.

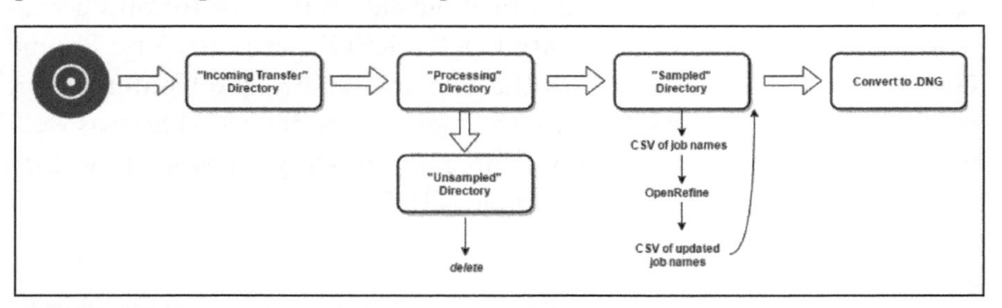

Figure 7.3 *Workflow at Johns Hopkins University with two automation steps* © Elizabeth England and Eric Hanson, Johns Hopkins University

Flexibility and more product, less process

In designing a workflow, flexibility may not come first to mind, but it is a critical goal. We are speaking here of the flexibility to adjust to diminished resources. This can occur for a number of reasons. You may encounter a technical problem with the material you are working with – an illegible file format for which you are obliged to spend a great deal of research time to try to understand it or play it back. Or it may be a simple reduction in staff, or a reduction in your own available time due to a new project you must address. Perhaps a department upon which you relied, a metadata team or the IT group, is no longer available to you in the capacity it previously was.

In all these cases, you want your workflows to continue to be guiding and usable documents. They should not contain sections that rely fully on a single step that you cannot reliably achieve. In most cases, this is easily sorted out. Very often steps *can* be skipped over and either returned to later or left as is.

This ability to adjust and continue processing work to reach the final goal of access, even under less-than-desirable resource availability, is discussed at length by Greene and Meissner (2005). The 'more product, less process' approach is initialised as MPLP, and it broadly addresses the ability to provide both user access and adequate care of materials in an institution's custody. This largely hinges on the ability to adjust processing practices as needed so as to move through received materials at a reasonable rate. For many collections, becoming entangled in the minutiae of processing born-digital materials is ultimately a disservice both to your users and to other materials which need processing attention.

Following this line of thinking, it is best to design workflows that can accommodate broader processing steps whenever necessary. This may include a much briefer descriptive phase for the received content, less curation in the presentation of the content for end-users, or a swifter scan for sensitive information, which correspondingly leaves more material inaccessible to the end-user until they request it – at which point you can conduct a more thorough evaluation of the flagged content. When you step back from your workflow, consider which parts of it are non-negotiable and absolutely must be completed. If your workflow is riddled with such parts, you may be conceiving of an overly rigid process that will not adjust well to changing conditions.

Workflow and policy

We have found that it is not untypical to encounter policy questions when designing a workflow. After all, workflows describe how you or your institution execute the professional actions for which it is responsible. To discover what those actions are, you will often need to consider your policy on one aspect or another. To put this another way, workflows naturally lead you to consider the principles guiding the actions described in the workflow. While it may seem incorrect to approach a high-level document policy from the standpoint of specific workflows, we think it is a natural outcome of workflow creation. However, we have put forward the same caveat that we introduced in the section on digital preservation policy in Chapter 5: while it is reasonable to reflect on policy when creating workflows, do not tie policy directly to specific workflow tools. Instead, consider the core function that the tools at hand are performing, and incorporate that function into the policy, rather than into the specific software or technique.

Examples

As we noted earlier, a group of workflows from a range of institutions tend to address similar work areas, but the action details quickly become particular to an institution as well. Fortunately, this means that example workflows are not just valuable for general framing, but also demonstrate solutions to specific decision points that you will encounter in born-digital processing. That decision point could include choices on item identifier creation (or the physical application method used for it), criteria for imaging a disk or simply copying files off, retention or disposal of the media, documentatioon of context or acquisition strategy – as well as numerous other decisions.

The Department of Rare Books and Special Collections at Princeton University Library hosts a sizeable collection of workflows that run from acquisition to processing, along with media-specific workflows for e-mail and web archiving (Princeton University, n.d.). Note, though, that the latter relies on the Archive-It service, which may limit its applicability if your institution is not using that service. Please note as well the number of workflows for processing alone, covering areas from device connection to file arrangement, description and virus scanning. We emphasise again the value of breaking down your process into manageable workflows.

The Digital Preservation Unit at Indiana University also provides a good deal of public-facing documentation on its processes at its *Born Digital Preservation Lab* website (Indiana University, n.d.). This runs from its own lab processes to ongoing work in repository certification. Under the former, take note of a Workflow Decision Matrix located on the website. This decision-based diagram can be an excellent way to navigate which workflows ought to be used for a given set of materials. The matrix addresses materials' properties such as the starting location of the content, whether the accession is ongoing or not, method of transfer, size and sensitive data. Depending on the answers to these questions, different workflows or processes may need to be used. You may consider drafting this type of document before you focus on the workflows themselves, as it may clarify how to divide your workflows.

Finally, the *Born Digital @ Yale* website hosts many posts, guides and workflows on handling born-digital materials (Yale, n.d.). Of particular interest here are the guides provided by the Digital Accessioning Service, with a workflow chart for accessioning born-digital materials and for disk image capture.

We expect that you will be able to locate guides provided by other institutions through your own searches, but the above guides can give you a good idea of the final outputs of the workflow process.

Case study

Before we conclude the chapter, let's take a look at a particular collection that illustrates some of the main points made here. In 2006, the Denver Art Museum (DAM) assumed stewardship of the American Institute for Graphic Arts (AIGA) award and recognition materials. As a professional organization committed to promoting design and designers, AIGA began recognising – and collecting – examples of exceptional design, starting in 1980. This set of material was given to DAM, and constitutes a wide range of media, including born-digital content on DVDs, CDs, USB flash drives and 3.5" floppy disks. In 2015, the museum was able to recruit new help to begin addressing the digital content on these carriers.

Let's look at the first steps. DAM set up a few key pieces of software and hardware to begin handling this material. The first component was the BitCurator suite of tools. BitCurator is a modified Linux environment that gathers many open source forensic tools for use in a cultural heritage setting. This environment would be used to run captures of the content once the media had been attached to the host computer. DAM also chose Archivematica to provide final processing and package management of the captured content. Archivematica is also a custom Linux environment, and this software was run on the same machine as BitCurator, inside of a virtual machine. This allowed for quicker use of the software without an immediate need to arrange a separate server.

Finally, the art conservator chose to use the KryoFlux floppy disk controller to capture content off the 3.5" disks, and a physical write blocker to help move content off the USB sticks. This initial outlay of tools allowed them to capture content from the media and send the disk images to Archivematica. Archivematica managed extraction of files from the disk images, identification of these files and generation of a final archival package, along with a standards-based descriptive file for this package.

Using only a few main tools, this strategy allowed the museum to capture all content from the media, and provides a very solid foundation to build upon. As you might expect, refinements to this strategy occurred as new challenges arose and needs changed. After an initial phase, Archivematica was moved from a machine local to the conservator to a server. Some of the optical media presented bad sectors and unique imaging problems, so the art conservator began using additional, media-specific software to supplement imaging in the BitCurator environment, packaging this additional material along with the captured content before processing in Archivematica.

As we mentioned earlier, a workflow is meant to be a dynamic document that can support adjustments to your process. This workflow also has the benefit of flexibility. For example, Archivematica need not receive a disk image; it may also process a directory of files, or a disk image that isn't mountable. Both of these conditions were present in the AIGA collection; some media was simply a transporting device that did not merit capture of a full sector copy, while some media was not mountable for file extraction, and will need further investigation at a later date. You can find a more in-depth description of this initial workflow online at the art conservator's own website (see the further reading section at the end of the chapter).

Conclusion

In this chapter we have covered both the value of workflows and strategies for generating them.

- Workflows are typically internally focused, but they can also be excellent communicative documents for outside parties.
- Breaking down workflows into manageable and logical component parts is a good approach to the project.
- We considered approaching workflows from an input–output or 'pipeline' approach, where every previous output becomes the input of the next step.

- We covered how workflows can accommodate the MPLP approach and general flexibility into their design.
- We noted that policy discussions and drafting are often a natural outcome of workflow generation.

Further reading

Archives of American Art (n.d.) *Internal Procedures and Guidelines*, www.aaa.si.edu/documentation.

The Archives of American Art has very usefully posted its own procedures online for ready viewing. Its section on Processing Guidelines in particular will be useful to you, as it is a great demonstration of workflows pointed to multiple audiences: a reference for its staff, professional material to share with others in the field and informative for the public as well. You will note as well that its processing guidelines explicitly take the MPLP advisements into account.

Colloton, E. (2015) *AGIA Electronic Media Survey for the Denver Art Museum*, http://eddycolloton.com/blog/2015/11/16/aiga-electronic-media-survey-for-the-denver-art-museum.

Here you can find a great, detailed look at a born-digital workflow being designed for a complex collection. Included are videos depicting some of the key pieces of software being used.

Novak Gustainis, E. R. (2012) Processing Workflow Analysis for Special Collections: the Center for the History of Medicine, Francis A. Countway Library of Medicine as case study, *RBM: A Journal of Rare Books, Manuscripts, and Cultural Heritage*, **13** (2), 113–28.

This article is a bit different from our other examples in the chapter, as it describes an *analysis* of existing workflows, rather than the generation of one. Nevertheless it is a good example of an institution's workflows, along with demonstrating the value that comes from reflecting on those workflows over time.

Prael, A. and Wickner, A. (2015) Getting to Know FRED: introducing workflows for born-digital content, *Practical Technology for Archives*, **4**, https://practicaltechnologyforarchives.org/issue4_prael_wickner/.

This article is an excellent demonstration of both a workflow and the process of discovering that workflow. Be sure to investigate the author's Appendix B to see a great full-scale diagram of their process.

CHAPTER 8

New and emerging areas in born-digital materials

The future has already happened.

(William Gibson, *Cyberpunk,* 1990)

New technologies are always being experimented with and tested. We want to take a moment here to look forward to developments in software, hardware and network technologies that may impact on how the cultural heritage field works with born-digital materials. Some of these topics will be technologies already in place and operating and some are only in early stages of testing and research. By 'looking forward', therefore, we mean both technologies on the possible horizon and existing technologies which you may wish to learn about further in your own exploration through this field.

Storage

Magnetic storage has been a dominant mode of information storage for decades, and its prominence continues today. However, new storage technologies are being explored and hold considerable promise for expanding further the amount of data we can store – and perhaps more importantly, increasing the efficiency with which we can do it.

Some of the new technologies being researched in labs are storage at the atomic level, spin transport electronics or 'spintronics', which encodes information according to the direction an electron is spinning (rather than the absence or presence of a charge), and data storage in DNA, using the sequences of the molecule's internal structure to retain digital information.

These are fascinating developments, but what does this mean for archives and libraries? Let's first bear in mind that we have already seen one revolution in data storage – from magnetic to solid state. Solid state technology is used in everything from laptops and desktops to SD cards, smartphones and USB sticks. The core technology is a grid of cells that can enclose individual electrons, maintaining the charge status of the cell even when the device is turned off.

Despite the fact that magnetic media and solid state are completely different strategies for retaining data, the manner in which you process a USB stick, as opposed to a spinning hard drive or floppy disk, is nearly identical. In both cases, you will probably attach that device to your host computer, perhaps use a write blocker, and attempt to take a full-sector copy of the device that includes the file system metadata and volume arrangement. When we are working with disk images we are operating at a level above that of the physical substrate of the media – we are capturing the stream of 0s and 1s with as much fidelity as we can. Those 0s and 1s are abstracted from the grid of cells or the plate of magnetic media. Along these lines, the interfaces we use to attach these devices are often the same, despite the radically different storage devices. Both a USB stick and an external spinning disk drive can be mediated by the USB interface, so the tools for one can apply to the other.

Nevertheless, these new technologies could greatly change how cultural heritage institutions do their work. Devices like the KryoFlux, which sample the flux differentials on a platter at a low level, are not applicable at all to solid state media, and that will certainly hold true for new media as well. In other words, the devices we use may change considerably if those devices are working with the media at a low enough level. Moreover, when we move from single storage devices that are part of a collection to the work of retaining large amounts of material in a preservation storage system, emerging research in new storage methods could change the landscape dramatically – from budgeting to redundancy and auditing strategies.

Software and apps

In this book, we have mostly talked about software as the set of tools you may use to manage born-digital content. However, there is another way in which software plays an important role in this area – as the preserved object itself. Software has arguably played *the* critical role in the evolution of computers and computing culture and it certainly plays an equal if not larger role in our lives today. From seminal pieces of productivity software, such as the spreadsheet programs VisiCalc and Lotus 1-2-3, to now ubiquitous word processing and e-mail clients, software is an important and looming marker of modern culture. That software will and should be in our cultural heritage collections seems very clear.

Certainly the scope does not stop at productivity programs. Video and computer games move many millions of units every year, and with the rise in smartphones and mobile games, computer games are arguably a part of more people's lives than at any previous time. In fact, the gaming community has played a critical role in software preservation and emulation tools as well. For example, DOSBox is a program designed to emulate the early, pre-Windows DOS environment common on IBM-PC compatibles in the 1980s and 1990s. While the initial intention was to provide a suitable environment for DOS games, it also works well as a general-purpose DOS environment in which to run vintage software that may come into your collection. The floppy disk controller KryoFlux was born out of the Software Preservation Society, a group focused on the preservation of vintage games on floppies.

As we move further into born-digital content management, it is likely we'll be relying increasingly on software run inside emulated or virtual environments, whether that is used to render back an older file or to run a piece of software itself. To this end, a good deal of work is being done in this area, from development of emulators to advocacy for rights to provide access to this software. A good starting place to learn more is the work of the Software Preservation Network, which features resources on technical implementation, standards, metadata and legal work.

With the rise of smartphones, 'apps', i.e. the software that is downloaded and run on the devices, are also in the ascendant. Unlike desktop software, however, apps present unique challenges because it is atypical for this software to be distributed on the internet. While this is true for both Android and iOS apps, it is much more the case for the latter, as Apple maintains central control over the distribution of software to iPhones through its App Store. In either case, however, it becomes significantly more difficult to preserve apps. Certainly, contact with the developers themselves is a possibility, but this still leaves a great deal uncovered, from the emulation frameworks that are more tightly bound to the smartphone hardware, to retention of previous versions of apps, along with the necessary advocacy to market forces for this immensely popular, but rarely preserved, domain of software.

Cloud technologies

We've given an introduction to forensics in the cultural heritage space in

Chapter 5, but what file system-level metadata can you retain when you do not have a file system on a carrier in front of you? This is the unique problem posed by cloud storage technologies. To be sure, this problem is most keenly felt at the moment by criminal forensics practices, which must still provide detailed, verifiable accounts of criminal activity to courts even when that activity is being conducted on remote servers. Nevertheless, it is reasonable to expect archives to encounter some version of this challenge as well when donors simply refer the institution to their Google Drive, Dropbox or OneDrive accounts.

If we are accustomed to having access to file creation times, last modified times and even other traces of user activity, such as partial data or deleted files, what affordances can we expect when capturing data from cloud storage locations? This is a fascinating problem area, and it would be best for the cultural heritage community to remain invested in adequate solutions for it.

Smartphones

We have touched on two technologies that swirl around the modern smartphone – cloud storage and apps – but not the device itself. Similar to the drive in a desktop computer, a smartphone constitutes a unique and arguably unparalleled locus of records and user activity, running from the personal (social media accounts, photos, notes, contact lists, music and other entertainment) to the professional and public (work documents and e-mail, professional networks and contacts) to everything in between (a great deal of browsing history). The archives field has already begun thinking about retention of records and other data on a smartphone.

For cultural heritage institutions, literature is scant at the moment on the best forensic technologies for attaching smartphones to a host machine for data capture. And while the archival value of a smartphone is apparent, it remains to be seen how willing users will be to donate their devices – perhaps the most personal of computers yet invented – to an institution. On top of this, smartphones are devices built from the ground up to be connected to the internet, and the level of coherence and completeness of the information retained on the device is always in flux. Arguably, an institution would be better served by seeking the germane accounts – e-mail, social media or other – than the devices in which the records from those accounts are sometimes present. Despite all this, a comprehensively preserved smartphone would make for a staggering insight into a user's habits, information management style, preferences and activities. This is certainly a space to continue monitoring!

Digital art and new media

About as soon as computers entered the realm of an individual's purchasing power, both professional artists and creatives began experimenting with them. From early electronic literature and poetry, to hyperlinked narratives, procedurally generated graphics and verse, web-based explorative sites and hybrid works relying on both physical materials and digital components, the range of new media containing born-digital components is too expansive to catalogue. Some of this creative output is sold commercially, some is freely available online and some is seen just in galleries and studios. Regardless of the venue, their preservation and representation to audiences over time is an ever-expanding challenge.

Some of the key hurdles here are the increased sensitivity to very fine details in aesthetics, the non-standard relationship between a digital component and a physical component, the complexity or relative obscurity of the software stack used to generate or present the art and a level of tolerance for variation in representation that the archives field is not always familiar with (or, to put this another way, the significant properties of a work are not always immediately clear).

To begin investigating this fascinating field of preservation, we suggest Richard Rinehart and Jon Ippolito's *Re-collection: art, new media, and social memory* (2014), which examines the preservation of new media art in excellent detail. For a look at this work in practice, check into the digital preservation program at the Rhizome arts organization, available online (http://rhizome.org).

Emerging descriptive and access methods

We've discussed how born-digital content puts forward unique considerations for description and access. As you might expect, there is work underway to develop technologies that might alleviate some of this work.

Emulation in your browser

We talked about emulation earlier, and one additional benefit to this access mode is the potential to run it through a user's browser. Instead of requiring the user to either run an emulator on their own machine or run that software on a reading-room machine, the user can simply view the requested resource in their own browser through an emulator that also runs in the browser. The best current example of this at work is the JSMESS project, which attempts to port the Multi Emulator Super System (MESS) to JavaScript (JS). JavaScript is a programming language that is found very frequently in the modern web, so a port of the MESS emulator to that language could facilitate a great deal of online access to vintage software. A great example of this is the Internet Archive's Internet Arcade, which features over 900 arcade video games emulated online.

Natural language processing

Description of born-digital content can be a challenge, due to the large corpus of text that a single hard drive, USB stick or CD could hold. What if there were some method to provide researchers with a finer description than we can do by manually scanning the documents listed on the screen? Natural language processing (NLP) is a work area that may promise such descriptions. The strategy here is to run algorithms on a body of text to identify important entities in the language – people, places, organizations or other concepts that would probably be of interest to researchers. In addition to assisting librarians and archivists with understanding the material they are processing, a reviewed list could provide users with a good idea of what they may find in a file or directory. This type of descriptive resource could be an excellent supplement to the traditional finding aid. NLP is being applied to a wide of range of subjects in a number of fields, but one example of this work in the archives field is BitCurator NLP, which is underway to provide NLP software for cultural heritage use.

Growing your skills

Now that we've covered a few interesting and promising developing areas for born-digital content, we want to bring the focus back to future developments for *you*. What are good ways to continue developing your knowledge and skills in the born-digital realm? Fortunately, the avenues for growth here are nearly limitless. Born-digital content constitutes a remarkably large and heterogeneous array of formats, media, software, environments and network technologies – all finding their way into cultural heritage institutions. We recognise, however, that the sheer number of potential areas to dive into can be overwhelming. Therefore, we've identified a few subjects here that we feel will be very useful to any practitioner, no matter what their particular interests or work scenarios.

Unix and scripting

As you continue working and studying in the born-digital field, you will find that Unix and Unix-like operating systems are the most common programming and development environment for a wide range of open source tools and packages. In fact, many of these tools do not feature graphic front ends and are instead accessible only through the Unix command line. Unix-like operating systems include all the various distributions of Linux (a few prominent ones being Ubuntu, Red Hat and CentOS), along with Apple's OS X and the more recent macOS systems. Since this is the case, familiarity and a basic comfort level with how Unix works and its underlying design philosophy are extremely useful. There is no shortage of books and resources on this subject, but we recommend two for you to consider first.

- Nemeth, E. et al. (2017) *UNIX and Linux System Administration Handbook*, Addison-Wesley.
- Strang, J. and Peek, J. (2001) *Learning the UNIX Operating System*, O'Reilly Media, Inc.

Along with the briefer *Unix in a Nutshell* recommended in Chapter 1, these books will ground you in the Unix environment and will prepare you to operate Linux and OS X or macOS machines with considerable skill. You'll learn about command line basics, command line text editors, the arrangement of system files, basic networking, security, package management and a host of other topics. We think you can't go wrong in becoming more knowledgeable in this area!

Closely tied to the command line skill is scripting. A script is a set of commands that you can write and execute in order to automatically run through a sequence of actions. A script can support a number of variations and branching paths, thereby supporting a considerable amount of logic inside it – or it can be quite straightforward, depending upon your needs. A script creates this chain of actions by using the commands and syntax of a command line shell, or by using the commands and functions of a programming language, such as Python, Perl or PHP.

A **shell** is a piece of software that allows a user to type commands into a computer. When you are at the command line of a Windows, Apple or Linux machine, you are inside a shell. You can almost think of a shell as a type of hovering spacecraft that allows you to interact with the planet below. Different spacecraft will have different operating instructions, but the planet below is always the same. Similarly, Linux and other operating systems can feature a number of shells with different affordances and conventions, but you are always working with the same underlying operating system. In Linux, a common shell is the **bash shell**. You can create whole scripts using only commands and syntax found in the bash shell, and save them all to a file; this is called shell scripting. If you are interested in shell scripting, decide which shell you'll be using, and look into tutorials and books on the subject.

Alternatively, you can use a programming language to generate your script. That programming language can avail itself of shell commands and conventions as well as its own functions and syntax. If you are interested in scripting with a programming language, decide which language you'll be using, and look into resources on scripting with it. No matter which method you choose, you'll be generating a set of actions that you can execute automatically to help you complete sets of commands very quickly. This is an immensely valuable skill that can allow you to perform actions in large batches, string together the inputs and outputs of numerous command line programs and automate some decision making.

Programming languages and coding

We have just mentioned programming languages in the context of generating a script – an executable set of instructions that runs as soon as you start it. But, you can also use programming language to create entire software programs or operating environments. This type of project is distinct from a script because it features more functions and interactions with the user, and needs to be compiled into executable code before being run on a computer. As you may guess, this is a considerably larger type of work with a correspondingly wider set of potential functions and applications. If you have ambitions to create entire programs – perhaps featuring a graphic interface – that you and others will use, learning even more about a programming language will set you on your way. In addition, ability with a programming language will put you in a position to contribute code to open source projects. While this skillset is probably less in demand in born-digital content work, it is a natural extension of familiarity with the command line and with scripting.

Web APIs

Finally, let's discuss APIs, and specifically APIs for web services. An API is a way for a user to interact with an application. Applications and services feature APIs so that the software can accommodate new user and developer needs, expanding the utility and value of the application or service. For example, Twitter offers an API to recall tweets, receive information on a user, search a hashtag and much more. This allows researchers to use these functions to conduct their work. If you use a third-party Twitter client, such Twitterrific or Tweetbot, you are using a piece of software that is deeply tied to the API of the Twitter service and that is making regular calls to the service through that API. Similar arrangements exist for other web services as well, and some software in the born-digital content space also features an API for you to use.

So, how do you take advantage of an API for a service you are interested in? Typically, you will begin calling the API functions through a programming language, similar to the manner in which you would put together a script. Instead of arranging commands from a shell or the programming language itself, you are primarily working with the functions and calls of the API. Once again, familiarity with a programming language will be of great use here. Facility with an API can allow you to make routine calls to a service or piece of software, and tie those calls into a larger workflow or script.

Conclusion

In this chapter, we have looked at emerging areas of born-digital preservation and access, and introduced a few areas for a practitioner to continue developing their skills.

- We covered how developments in storage can affect acquisition and forensic practices, noting how the physical substrate of storage does and does not play into this work.
- We discussed the value and the challenges in preserving software and mobile apps, and how the landscape changes when that software is distributed over the internet or through proprietary app stores.
- We examined some of the challenges in preserving data located in the cloud and on smartphones.
- Similarly, we talked about unique issues in new media digital art and the complexity of significant properties there.

- We also covered emulation as a service online, and the potential of NLP to aid description.
- Finally, we introduced three areas to further develop knowledge: Unix operation, scripting and programming, and web API use.

Further reading

Kirschenbaum, M. (2008) *Mechanisms: new media and the forensic imagination*, MIT Press.

We touched on storage technologies in this chapter, noting that in many cases the level of abstraction between the physical technology and the software technology allows the practitioner to retain workflows despite varying storage mediums. However it is well worth your while to dig into the physical details of storage (and computing in general), and Matthew Kirschenbaum's book on forensics, storage and the physical mechanisms behind storage is a wonderful way to do so. The author grounds his text in real explorations of computer games, disk images and electronic literature, and this will give you a great grasp of why forensics are critical to cultural heritage work – along with how the physicality of computing informs our practices.

McDonough, J. et al. (2010) *Preserving Virtual Worlds Final Report*, Library of Congress.

Proximate to digital art and new media are video games (and more broadly, all genres of software). Great work has already been done in this area, from emulation to documentation and disk image preservation. This 2010 report is an excellent summary of such work, examining titles as far back as the text games *Adventure* (1977) and more modern hits like *Warcraft III* (2002) or open-ended virtual worlds like *Second Life* (2003). The authors consider dependencies, significant properties and intellectual property law, as well as deliberating on what exactly constitutes a game and virtual world. Games and virtual worlds are fascinating notions that can end up functioning as object, activity and community all at once, so their preservation is a very rich space to explore.

Rinehart, R. and Ippolito, J. (2014) *Re-collection: art, new media, and social memory*, MIT Press.

If the problems and strategies in new media and digital art interest you, *Re-collection* is a fantastic examination of the challenges in this area, covering the technical hurdles and affordances, how law (copyright and other domains) affects preservation strategies, and the relationship between the digital objects produced and the institutions assigned to retaining and representing them. Similar to Kirschenbaum's *Mechanisms*, the authors move through these areas with specific case studies.

Conclusion

> The best of my nature reveals itself in play, and play is sacred.
> (Karen Blixen, *On Modern Marriage and Other Observations*, 1987, 80)

Now that you've made your way through the book we hope that you feel confident enough to embark on some born-digital content management, and to start the long and exciting journey of learning and growing as the technology we use to record knowledge shifts and changes over time. Now that we've whetted your appetite, we encourage you to take a look at the additional resources in Appendix A for more avenues to explore. We wholeheartedly encourage you to pick up more computer programming skills if that's a path that interests you. If it doesn't, that's fine too.

The fact that you picked up this book indicates you have at least an interest in the subject, which is half the battle. We want to emphasise that having strong computer programming and technological skills is not imperative in order to be a good born-digital content manager. You need to have the basic knowledge of the challenge, to find the right people who can help you and to communicate with them what you need to happen and why. We hope that we have shared with you enough of the fundamental knowledge you will need in order to do this and to guide you in the direction of more information that you can pick up as you go.

After reading this book you should know a little bit more about the basics of how digital information is created and rendered, and about born-digital-specific practices around selection, acquisition, description, preservation and access – how to tie all of these elements together; and a little bit about what may lie ahead.

In Chapter 1 you learned about the range of methods by which words, numbers, images, sound and videos are encoded into the binary information that computers are designed to interpret and render in various ways. We considered a number of different digital file formats and looked closely at how binary information is encoded on different types of physical media. In that chapter we also introduced some basic information about the command line and how you might use it in your practice. Understanding these very basic concepts will help you to understand the root of all of the decisions you will be making throughout the full spectrum of born-digital content management.

The first of these decisions was covered in Chapter 2, on selection. We explored the most likely types of digital content that you could acquire in your library or archives, and we looked at the different factors to consider when deciding which content you should acquire. These involve the collection policies that stem from your institution's mission statement. As the step between selection and acquisition, we included information about donor agreements that address born-digital acquisitions.

We covered the acquisition process in detail in Chapter 3, in addition to accessioning (in archival environments) and ingesting (in libraries and repository environments). We discussed in detail the numerous processes that you should consider incorporating into your accessioning and ingest workflows. We introduced write blockers, disk drives, floppy disk controllers, disk images, physical carriers, checksums, network-born content, web archiving, e-mail collecting and considerations for collecting social media. The chapter was quite extensive and you should now have a very good grasp of the core work of immediately handling born-digital content.

Selecting and acquiring your born-digital content is a very involved process, but it is only the beginning of your work of managing this content. You must also develop systems to properly describe your content so that you can identify it and maintain the records that are important in order to manage it over time. In Chapter 4, we covered the various types of information that you will need to collect that are specific to born-digital content. We examined a number of descriptive standards that you may adopt or adapt for this purpose and introduced some of the descriptive systems that are currently available to record this information.

Once you've acquired and described your content, you need to take measures to preserve your ability to access it over time. In Chapter 5, you learned the important distinction between an environment built for the creation and access of digital content at an individual level, the types of storage systems we create for the organisation and preservation of conent in our libraries and archives. You also learned about file formats and storage and the importance of storing several replicated versions of your content in different locations. We covered fixity checks in the context of mass storage, budgeting, certification, policies and, perhaps most importantly, making the case for focused digital preservation services in your institution.

You must also have picked up on the fact that there is no preservation without access, just as there is no access without preservation. Really, what's the point of preserving the content if, even sometime far in the future, no one can access it? We covered the importance of and approaches to providing access to your born-digital content in Chapter 6. We also discussed some of the things you may encounter that will prevent you from providing open access to your content, such as copyrights, digital rights protection mechanisms, password-protected and otherwise encrypted files, and the numerous laws that protect the privacy of personally identifying, medical and education information. Though some of the technology we discussed will change over time, we presented some of the current systems that you can use to provide access to your content.

Up to this point in the book, we had presented all of the basic components of managing born-digital content, and in Chapter 7 we helped you to put all of those elements together into some overarching workflows. We looked at tools, design principles, potential audience and procedures related to putting together your own workflows. We explored automation and examined the difference between open source, interoperable and non-proprietary software and how these differences may affect how you design your workflow.

Just when you thought you had learned everything you possibly could about managing born-digital content, in Chapter 8 we took you on a short journey into the future. Since born-digital content is born (pardon the pun) out of technological advances, we always have to be looking ahead at upcoming changes, both known and otherwise. We took a quick look at advances in storage, software and apps, cloud technologies, smartphones, digital art and new media, emerging descriptive and access methods, emulation in your browser and natural language processing. We also looked at your future and suggested some additional skills you can pick up to help you keep up with these changes. We know that we can't predict everything, and we fully expect some surprises ahead. But that's what makes this work so exciting! We don't *really* know what's going to happen down the road, so we know that there will always be new and interesting challenges to keep us thinking and engaged with the work.

Something that remains a question, however, is who you are and what has drawn you to this line of work. Why do you want to learn about managing born-digital collections? What interests you about it? For decades, would-be librarians and archivists were drawn to the profession first for the knowledge, but second for a visceral love of books and old documents. We loved to hold the books and pieces of history in our hands and breathe in that dusty vanilla scent. But now the nature of the material is changing. That's not to say that our beloved books and old documents are going away, but what may have drawn people to the profession is shifting.

Most of what we work with, if not now, will soon be mostly digital. More than that, it will be born-digital content. Beyond a passion for preserving and providing access to the outputs and creations of humanity, what is it that will draw people to the field? It certainly can't be the smell, right? Will it be the love for technological challenges? The thrill of unexplored territory? Could it be nostalgia, or even a curiosity, about technologies from 30 or 40 years ago? We know that there are groups of individuals enchanted with playing video games from the 1980s and who work tirelessly to try to preserve them. As we mentioned earlier, the KryoFlux, one of the tools we use for creating disk images of old floppy disks, was created by a group of video game enthusiasts in Germany.

The future is wide open for this kind of work. It is unequivocally important work, and we may be facing a day when the phrase 'born-digital' does not serve as a modifier to library or archives, and we will no longer have digital librarians and digital archivists, but professionals focused on different media and content areas as we are largely organized now.

Clearly this is a conclusion that is not definitive, only provisional. Questions persist for the future: the types of content for which we will steward the modes of access and use that our users will want, and the changes our institutions will need to undergo.

William Shakespeare wrote in *The Tempest*, 'How beauteous mankind is! O brave new world, That has such people in't!' It is quite the brave new world we are in, and it's getting braver and newer every day. We can look at this quote from Aldous Huxley's viewpoint as well, where the so-called brave new world is full of uncontrolled and unruly advances that plague society. Our work managing born-digital collections is proof that, while advances in technology genuinely enhance and expand our ability to create, share and discover new creations, they also makes it infinitely more difficult to collect and preserve access over the long-term, or to even evaluate what is worth saving. That's not to say that we can't continue our professional mission into the digital era – we believe we absolutely can.

In the quote at the beginning of this section, Karen Blixen reflects on the importance of play, or in her words, the sacredness of play. Play is perhaps one of the most integral pieces of figuring things out. It is with playfulness that we poke and prod at puzzles and watch what happens as a result. In all seriousness, it must be with playfulness that we move into and through the ever shifting landscape that our professions are becoming. It is through states of playfulness and playful curiosity that we will work through the challenges that continue to evolve before us and build the new knowledge and skills that we need in order to collect, preserve and provide access to our collective digital histories.

References

Bailey, J. (2012) Partly Cloudy: trends in distributed and remote preservation storage – more results from the NDSA storage survey, *The Signal*, https://blogs.loc.gov/thesignal/2012/01/partly-cloudy-trends-in-distributed-and-remote-preservation-storage-more-results-from-the-ndsa-storage-survey/.

BitCurator Consortium (n.d.) *Acquire – Create Disk Images*, BitCurator Environment Documentation, https://confluence.educopia.org/display/BC/Acquire.

Blixen, K. (1987) *On Modern Marriage and Other Observations*, London: Fourth Estate.

Carolina Digital Repository (2018) CDR Collection Development Policy, http://blogs.lib.unc.edu/cdr/index.php/about/policies-guidelines/cdr-collection-development-policy/.

Connecticut State Library (1996) Collection Policy for the State Archives in the Connecticut State Library, https://ctstatelibrary.org/collection-policy-state-archives-con.

Cooper, N. (2012) The Invisible Neutron Threat, *National Security Science*, **1**, www.lanl.gov/science/NSS/issue1_2012/story4full.shtml.

England, E. and Hanson, E. (2017) Automating Digital Archival Processing at Johns Hopkins University, *The Signal*, https://blogs.loc.gov/thesignal/2017/05/automating-digital-archival-processing-at-johns-hopkins-university/.

Gibson, W. (1990) *Cyberpunk*, video, directed by Marianne Trench, New York: Intercon Production.

Gordon, B. and Arnold, H. (2015) Arrangement and Description for Born-digital Materials, *CURATECamp* 2015, www.slideshare.net/slideshow/embed_code/key/3NvGNKvW9BeFa8.

Greene, M. and Meissner, D. (2005) More Product, Less Process: revamping traditional archival processing, *The American Archivist*, **68** (2) (Fall/Winter), 208–63.

Hillis, D. (1998) *The Pattern on the Stone: the simple ideas that make computers work*, New York: Basic Books.

Indiana University (n.d.) *Born Digital Preservation Lab*, https://wiki.dlib.indiana.edu/display/DIGIPRES/Born+Digital+Preservation+Lab.

Irish Architectural Archive (2016) Acquisitions Policy Statement, www.iarc.ie/wp-content/uploads/2016/08/IAA-Accessions-Policy-2016.pdf.

Jefferson, T. (1791) From Thomas Jefferson to Ebenezer Hazard, 18 February 1791, *Founders Online*, National Archives, last modified 26 November, 2017, http://founders.archives.gov/documents/Jefferson/01-19-02-0059. [Original source: *The Papers of Thomas Jefferson*, vol. 19, *24 January–31 March 1791*, ed. Julian P. Boyd. Princeton: Princeton University Press, 1974, 287–9.]

Kelly, K. (2010) *What Technology Wants*, New York: Viking Penguin.

Kirschenbaum, M. (2008) *Mechanisms: new media and the forensic imagination*, MIT Press.

Massachusetts Institute of Technology (1976) Institute Archives Records Collection Policy, https://libraries.mit.edu/archives/managing/policy-collection.html.

Muncaster, P. (2012) HDD Oligopoly to Keep Post-flood Prices High Till 2014, *The Register*, www.theregister.co.uk/2012/06/07/thai_floods_prices_2014/.

Noonan, D. (2014) Digital Preservation Policy Framework: a case study, *EDUCASE Review*, https://er.educause.edu/articles/2014/7/digital-preservation-policy-framework-a-case-study.

Pearson, D. and Webb, C. (2008) Defining File Format Obsolescence: a risky journey, *International Journal of Digital Curation*, **3** (1), https://doi.org/10.2218/ijdc.v3i1.44.

Princeton University (n.d.) *Born-Digital Workflows*, https://rbsc.princeton.edu/workflows/born-digital.

Rosenthal, D. (2009) Spring CNI Plenary: The Remix, *DSHR's Blog*, http://blog.dshr.org/2009/04/spring-cni-plenary-remix.html.

Rosenthal, D. (2016) The Medium-Term Prospects for Long-Term Storage Systems, *DSHR's blog*, http://blog.dshr.org/2016/12/the-medium-term-

prospects-for-long-term.html.
Rosenthal, D., Robertson, T., Lipkis, T., Reich, V. and Morabito, S. (2005) Requirements for Digital Preservation Systems: a bottom-up approach, *D-Lib Magazine*, **11** (11), www.dlib.org/dlib/november05/rosenthal/11rosenthal.html.
Scott, J. (2011) Floppy Disks: it's too late, *ASCII blog*, http://ascii.textfiles.com/archives/3191.
Sheldon, M. (2013) Analysis of Current Digital Preservation Policies: archives, libraries and museums, *The Signal*, https://blogs.loc.gov/thesignal/2013/08/analysis-of-current-digital-preservation-policies-archives-libraries-and-museums/.
University of Alabama Birmingham Libraries (n.d.) UAB Digital Collections Policies, https://library.uab.edu/locations/digital-collections/policies-digital-collections.
University of Leicester University Library (2016) Archives Collections Management Policy, www2.le.ac.uk/library/downloads/collection-policies/special-collections-policy.
University of Victoria Libraries (n.d.) Archives Collections Policy, www.uvic.ca/library/locations/home/archives/archival_resources/collections_policy.php.
Weinberger, D. (2007) *Everything is Miscellaneous*, New York: Times Books.
Williams, D. R. and Bell, E. (2016) NASA Space Science Data Coordinated Archive Mission Statement, https://nssdc.gsfc.nasa.gov/about/charter.html.
World Digital Library (n.d.), www.wdl.org/en/.
Yale University (n.d.) *Born Digital @ Yale*, https://guides.library.yale.edu/borndigital.

Appendix A: Resources

Now that your appetite for learning about born-digital content has been properly whetted, we imagine that you would like to know the best resources available to you to learn more. Here we provide information about books, journals, technical registries, generally helpful websites and, perhaps most importantly, communities of practice that you can reach out to in order to expand your knowledge and capabilities. A few of the resources listed below are repeated from the further reading sections at the end of each chapter, but we have done so because we believe they are valuable enough to gather into this overarching resource section.

Books

Books (like this one!) are a great place to pick up some basic knowledge that you can later put into practice. While this is currently the only book for cultural heritage practitioners that is focused solely on born-digital content, we suggest a number of books that provide supporting knowledge to this focus.

- Ambacher, B. I. (ed.) (2003) *Thirty Years of Electronic Records*, Scarecrow Press, Inc.
- Brown, A. (2006) *Archiving Websites: a practical guide for information management professionals*, Facet Publishing.
- Brown, A. (2013) *Practical Digital Preservation: a how-to guide for organizations of any size*, Facet Publishing.
- Carrier, B. (2005) *File System Forensic Analysis*, Addison-Wesley.
- Delve, J. and Anderson, D. (eds) (2014) *Preserving Complex Digital Objects*, Facet Publishing.
- Dobreva, M. (ed.) (forthcoming, 2018) *Digital Archives: management, access and use*, Facet Publishing.

- Friedl, J. E. F. (2006) *Mastering Regular Expressions*, O'Reilly Media, Inc.
- Kirschenbaum, M. (2008) *Mechanisms: new media and the forensic imagination*, MIT Press.
- Lowdermilk, T. (2013) *User-centered Design*, O'Reilly Media, Inc.
- Marshall, B. H. (ed.) (2017) *The Complete Guide to Personal Digital Archiving*, Facet Publishing.
- Millar, L. (2017) *Archives: principles and practices*, 2nd edn, Facet Publishing.
- Oliver, G. and Harvey, R. (2016) *Digital Curation*, 2nd edn, Facet Publishing.
- White, R. (2014) *How Computers Work: the evolution of technology*, 10th edn, Que Publishing.

Journals

Journals can provide more current reports on specific topics. They can sometimes provide more in-depth analysis on technical subjects. The journals listed below often publish articles relevant to born-digital content, and have at times published issues with a born-digital theme.

- *American Archivist*
- *Archivaria*
- *Archives and Records: The Journal of the Archives and Records Association*
- *Code4Lib Journal*
- *International Journal of Digital Curation*
- *Journal of Digital Information*
- *Proceedings of the International Conference on Digital Preservation*

Reports

Like journals, reports can provide more up-to-date information. They often present deep-dives on useful topics, and can also present useful technical tit-bits. Start with the reports listed below and take a look at their reference sections for additional resources.

- AIMS Workgroup (2012) *AIMS Born-digital Collections: an inter-institutional model for stewardship*, https://dcs.library.virginia.edu/files/2013/02/AIMS_final_text.pdf.

- Blue Ribbon Task Force (2010) *Sustainable Economics for a Digital Planet: ensuring long-term access to digital information, Final Report of the Blue Ribbon Task Force on Sustainable Digital Preservation and Access*, http://brtf.sdsc.edu/biblio/BRTF_Fkinal_Report.pdf.
- Consultative Committee for Space Data Systems (2011) *Audit and Certification for Trustworthy Digital Repositories*, CCSDS Secretariat, https://public.ccsds.org/pubs/652x0m1.pdf.
- Consultative Committee for Space Data Systems (2012) *Reference Model for an Open Archival Information System*, CCSDS Secretariat, https://public.ccsds.org/pubs/650x0m2.pdf.
- Phillips, M., Bailey, J., Goethals, A. and Owens, T. (2013) *The NDSA Levels of Digital Preservation: an explanation and uses*, Library of Congress, www.digitalpreservation.gov/documents/NDSA_Levels_Archiving_2013.pdf.
- Redwine, G., Barnard, M., Donovan, K., Farr, E., Forstrom, M., Hansen, W., Leighton John, J., Kuhl, N., Shaw, S. and Thomas, S. (2013) *Born Digital: guidance for donors, dealers, and archival repositories*, Council on Library and Information Resources, www.clir.org/wp-content/uploads/sites/6/pub159.pdf.

Technical registries

Technical registries are the best places to find technical specification information about digital storage media, file formats and other hardware and software. As you can see, there are quite a few of these types of registries. Most of the common formats are described in these registries, and a number of the less-common formats as well.

- Digital Preservation Technical Registry
- Just Solve the File Format Problem
- Library of Congress Sustainability of Digital Formats
- MediaPedia
- OPF Format Corpus
- PRONOM

Websites

At the time of writing, there are a number of websites that were created to collect and share valuable information on born-digital content and related topics. Check out the websites listed below to collect some useful information.

- Core Trust Seal (recently took over for Data Seal of Approval certification activities), www.coretrustseal.org/.
- Demystifying Born Digital web page from OCLC Research, www.oclc.org/research/themes/research-collections/borndigital.html.
- Digital Preservation Management tutorials, www.dpworkshop.org/.
- Library of Congress's Sustainability of Digital Formats, www.loc.gov/preservation/digital/formats/.

Conferences

Conferences that are known to support research and practice around born-digital content are fabulous places not only to pick up some knowledge and a few handy pointers, but also to connect with others who are working on similar problems. Take a look at the annual conferences listed below and see if any spark your interest.

- Best Practices Exchange (BPE)
- Chartered Institute of Library and Information Professionals Conference
- Coalition for Network Information
- Code4Lib
- CURATECamp
- Digital Library Federation Forum
- International Conference on Digital Preservation (iPres)
- International Digital Curation Conference (IDDC)
- Preservation and Archiving Special Interest Group (PASIG)

Communities

Communities of practice are probably going to be one of your most valuable resources. You can start with regional organizations nearby, like your regional library or archives organization group. Chances are, there will be others nearby who are working on similar issues. To supplement your local networks, you can also look to some of the groups listed below. They are populated by skilled, experienced people who are more than happy to share their knowledge.

- BitCurator Consortium
- Data Archiving and Networked Services
- DigiPres Commons
- Digital Preservation Coalition
- DigitalPreservationEurope
- Electronic Records Section of the Society of American Archivists
- International Internet Preservation Consortium (IIPC)
- National Digital Stewardship Alliance
- nestor
- Open Preservation Foundation
- Research Data Alliance

Appendix B: Basic Unix command line prompts

Not knowing how to operate in command line interfaces will not prevent you from effectively working with born-digital content, but it will certainly slow you down. There are a great many very useful guides to using the command line, and lists of the hundreds of commands that are at your disposal – both online and in print. We present to you here a list of some of the most basic Unix commands that you can use, to give you a sense of some of the commands you may want to use. You can use these Unix commands on most Apple computers and in the Windows 10 platform. Most of these commands have numerous optional variables that you will want to specify when you put them to use. You can find information for these variables online or in references like Arnold Robbins' *Unix in a Nutshell,* listed in the further reading of Chapter 1 – or you can use the `whatis` command in your command line to display brief descriptions of the command and its available options.

`*` The wildcard `*` selects all of the files in the current directory.

`cd` Stands for 'change directory' where 'directory' is what you may know as a 'folder' on your computer. Type `cd` and then the name of the directory or the directory path that you would like to go to, to move into a different directory.

`cd ..` Allows you to move up one directory from your current location, without having to type out the directory name or the whole path to the directory.

`chmod` Changes the access mode for specified files. You can specify variables for this command to allow or prevent read, write or execute abilities for specified users or groups of users.

`chown` Changes the ownership of specified files.

`cksum` A handy command that calculates a cyclic redundancy check

	(CRC) for specified files. You can use the default algorithm or specify others.
`cmp`	Allows you to compare files to determine if they are identical, different or inaccessible.
`cp`	Copies files or directories.
`curl`	Retrieves files from the internet using FTP or HTTP. You may run into this command when working through installation processes of open source software.
`df`	Reports the number of free disk blocks on mounted file systems.
`diff`	Reports which lines are different between two different files.
`du`	Shows the disk usage for the specified directory.
`emacs`	Runs the Emacs text editor.
`file`	Can be used for basic file format identification using the 'magic file' information.
`find`	Useful for finding files or groups of files.
`finger`	Displays information about users.
`ftp`	Transfers files from a remote network to a specified site.
`grep`	Stands for 'global regular expression print'. It searches files matching patterns and returns the results. This is the command commonly used to execute regular expression string searches that we describe in Chapter 6.
`groups`	Shows the groups to which a user belongs.
`gzip`	Compresses files or groups of files into a smaller package.
`head`	Prints the first few lines of specified files.
`hexdump`	Prints out the digital file in hexadecimal, octal, decimal or ASCII format.
`home`	The HOME variable is an environment variable that displays the path of the home directory.
`hostname`	Sets or prints the name of the current host system.
`iconv`	Converts the content of a file from one character set to another.
`info`	Shows available documentation for specified directories or files.
`kill`	Terminates specified processes by ID (identification).
`ldd`	Lists 'dynamic dependencies', meaning that it lists all files that would be loaded, should the file be executed.
`login`	Signs you into the system.

`logname`	Displays your login name.
`lp`	Sends files to the printer.
`ls`	Lists all files and directories in the working directory.
`man`	Displays an online reference manual.
`mkdir`	Creates directories.
`mount`	Mounts a specified file system.
`mv`	Moves files from one specified directory location to another.
`passwd`	Creates or changes passwords for specified users.
`pwd`	Prints the full pathname of the current directory. Stands for 'print working directory', not to be confused with the `passwd` command.
`rm`	Deletes specified files.
`rmdir`	Deletes specified directories.
`scp`	Securely copies files between hosts on a network using `ssh`.
`script`	Creates a record of your login session.
`sftp`	Allows you to securely transfer files to a host site.
`size`	Displays the size of a specified file in bytes.
`ssh`	Securely logs a user into a remote system.
`tar`	Takes multiple files or directories and packages them as one file.
`touch`	Updates access and modification timestamps to the current time and date for specified files.
`umount`	Unmounts a filesystem.
`uname`	Shows the current Unix system name.
`unix2dos`	Converts a file's ISO standard characters to DOS counterparts.
`unzip`	Decompresses or 'opens' a ZIP archive.
`users`	Shows which users are currently logged in to the system.
`vi`	Runs the vi text editor.
`vim`	Runs the vim text editor.
`whatis`	Looks up and shows a brief description for specified commands.
`zip`	Takes multiple files or directories and packages them as one file.

Index

3D images 18
3D modelling, animation and rendering software 32

AACR (Anglo-American Cataloguing Rules) 91–3, 94, 101
access and access strategies 129–30
  accessibility 138–9
  emerging access methods 169–70
  hardware and software considerations 130–3
  hybrid collections 142–3
  legal and copyright restrictions 133–5
  network-born media 140
  online access and platforms 145–7
  on-site access 147–8
  original order 54, 139–42, 143
  remote and restricted online access 147
  significant properties 137–8
  technological infrastructure 144–5
  technological restrictions 135–6
  third-party materials in arrangement and context 143–4
accessibility 138–9
accessioning digital media 44, 53, 83–4 (*see also* deaccessioning digital media)
acquisition 53
  checksums and checksum algorithms 69–71
  disk images and the file system 62–3
  e-mail 78–81, 112, 134
  file extraction and examination 63–9
  file system 55–6
  on-demand capture 76–8
  principles 53–4
  social media 81–3, 112
  web archives 78
  web crawlers 74–6
  websites 71–4
  write blocking 56–61
AIP (Archival Information Package) 121–2
American Institute for Graphic Arts (AIGA) 161–2

American Standard Code for Information Interchange *see* ASCII
Anglo-American Cataloguing Rules *see* AACR
API (application programming interface) 82, 83–4
  web APIs 173
Apple File System (APFS) 56
application programming interface *see* API
apps, preservation of 35, 167 (*see also* mobile devices; smartphones)
Archival Information Package *see* AIP
Archive-It (on-demand capture) 47– 8, 77, 160
Archivematica (file extraction software) 64, 114, 157, 161, 162
archives
  descriptive standards 95–9
  descriptive systems 101–6
  web 46–9, 71–8
Archives New Zealand 37
ArchivesSpace 103, 104, 157
Archives Unleashed Project 74
ASCII (American Standard Code for Information Interchange) 10–12, 65, 98
audio recordings 18–19, 33
automation (workflow design) 157–8 (*see also* input and output pipeline)

BagIt (open packaging specification) 84
Bézier curve 17(*see also* vector images)
BIBFRAME 94
bibliographic descriptive standards 90–4
bibliographic descriptive systems 102
binary information 9–12
  hex editors 64
  images 13–16, 17, 19
  magnetic media 23, 24
  optical media 24, 25
  solid-state storage 25
  spreadsheets 20
BitCurator environment 134, 156, 161, 162
  BitCurator Access (online access platform) 146
  BitCurator Disk Image Access Tool (file extraction software) 64, 114
  BitCurator NLP 170
bitmapped images 13–16
Blue Ribbon Task Force, report on economic challenges of digital preservation 120, 121
books, selection of 33
born-digital-specific collection policies 42–3
budgeting, digital preservation and storage 118–20

Carolina Digital Repository, collection development policy 43
CD-ROMs *see* optical media
certification for digital preservation storage

CoreTrustSeal 123
Open Archival Information System (OAIS) 121–2
checksums and checksum algorithms 69–71, 88, 117 (*see also* fixity data; PREMIS)
cloud technologies 167–8
code repositories 9
GitHub 28, 29, 63
Sourceforge 28
collection policies 37
born-digital-specific policies 42–3
Carolina Digital Repository's collection development policy 43
Connecticut State Library Archives' Collection Policy 41
content-driven policy statements 40–1
Irish Architectural Archive's acquisitions policy 42–3
Massachusetts Institute of Technology. Institute Archives and Special Collections, Records
Collection Policy 40–1
policies excluding digital content 43–4
policies including digital content 41–2
Stanford University, collection development guidance for web archiving 46–9
University of Alabama at Birmingham (UAB) Libraries Digital Collections policy 42
University of Leicester Library's collecting policy 43–4
University of Victoria Libraries' collections policy 41
(*see also* mission statements)
command line operations 26–8, 75–6, 157–8, 171, 193–5 (*see also* scripting; write blocking)
computer and video games 32, 35–6, 167, 170, 180
Connecticut State Library Archives, collections policy 41
conservation treatments 89–90
CONTENTdm (digital content management system) 44, 103, 146
content-driven policy statements 40–1
copyrights and licensing (access) 89, 133–5
CoreTrustSeal (digital preservation certification process) 123
creation and revision dates or timestamps 88

DACS (Describing Archives: A Content Standard) 95, 97–8, 103, 104
Dartmouth College Library's Digital Preservation Policy 125–6
databases 20–2, 33, 140
data visualisation 36
deaccessioning digital media 44, 66–8 (*see also* accessioning digital media)
Denver Art Museum (DAM), workflow example 161–2

Describing Archives: A Content Standard *see* DACS
description of born-digital content, types of information
access codes and encryption keys 89
conservation treatments 89–90
copyrights and licensing 89, 133–5
creation and revision dates or timestamps 88
emerging descriptive and access methods 169–70
file types and formats 88
fixity data 88
hardware 88–9
linked or associated files 89
personally identifying information (PII) 89, 133, 134
physical media information 89
rendering software 88
(*see also* descriptive standards; descriptive systems; element sets)
descriptive standards
archives 95–9
bibliographic 90–4
and element sets 90, 101, 102
descriptive systems 101
archival 102–3
bibliographic 102
digital preservation systems 103
digital repositories 103
and element sets 101, 102
digital art and new media 169
digital documents, selection of 33
digital images, selection 34
digital preservation and storage 144
budgeting 118–20
certification 121–3
communicating the need for preservation 120–1
Dartmouth College Library's Digital Preservation Policy 125–6
file format obsolescence 113
fixity checks and auditing 116–17
long-lived media 117–18
models 126–7
policy 123–7
replication 115–16
roles, responsibilities and collaboration 125–6
software 35, 167
digital repositories 103, 115–16
digital storage media 22–3
magnetic 23–4, 165–6
optical 24–5
solid-state storage media 25–6, 165–6
digital watermarking 130, 135, 136, 149
disk imaging 62–3, 166, 167
Dissemination Information Package *see* DIP
Dissemination Information Package (DIP) 121–2
donor agreements 37, 53, 54, 148–9 (*see also* gift agreements)
Drupal (online access platform) 146

DSpace (online access platform) 146
Dublin Core (element set) 42, 100, 103 (*see also* metadata; PREMIS)
DVDs *see* optical media

e-books, selection 33–4
editors
  Emacs 27, 28, 194
  Hex 64–5
  Vim 27, 28, 195
electronic journals, selection 34
element sets
  Dublin Core 100
  PREMIS 100–1
e-mail 2
  access 146
  acquisition 78–81, 112, 134
  management and processing software 81
  selection 34
Emacs editor 27, 28, 194
emerging descriptive and access methods 169–70
Emory University Manuscript, Archives, and Rare Books Library 132, 148
emulation 167, 169–70
encoding systems
  ASCII (American Standard Code for Information Interchange) 10–12, 65, 98
  hexadecimal 11, 12, 64, 65
  Unicode standard 12, 17
encryption 89, 130, 136
ePADD (email management and processing software) 81, 134, 146

feed lists and playlists, selection 35
File Allocation Table (FAT) (file system) 24, 55
file extraction and examination

  acquisition 63–9
  software 64, 114, 157, 161, 162
file formats 42, 88, 112–14 (*see also* audio recordings; databases; e-mail; images; spreadsheets; video; websites)
file systems
  Apple File System (APFS) 56
  and disk images 62–3
  File Allocation Table (FAT) 24, 55
  first, second, third and fourth extended file systems 56
  Hierarchical File System (HFS) 56
  New Technology File System (NTFS) 55
  for optical media 25
  for solid-state storage 26
first, second, third and fourth extended file systems 56
fixity data 88, 116–17 (*see also* checksums and checksum algorithms; PREMIS)
floppy disks 53, 57–9, 60–1
forensic bridge *see* write blocking
Forestry Research Institute of Ghana Library, mission statement 38

format versus content-driven collecting decisions 36–7

General International Standard Archival Description *see* ISAD(G)
gift agreements 44
  University of Colorado Boulder Special Collections, Archives and Preservation Gift Agreement 44–6 (*see also* donor agreements)
GitHub (code repository) 28, 29, 63
graphical user interface (GUI) 26, 27, 28

hardware and software considerations (access) 88–9, 130–3
Harry Ransom Center 141
hexadecimal (encoding system) 11, 12, 64, 65
hex editors 64–6
HFSExplorer (file extraction software) 64
Hierarchical File System (HFS) 56
HTML (HyperText Markup Language) 22, 72
HTTrack (web crawler) 75
hybrid collections, access 142–3
HyperText Markup Language *see* HTML

identifiers for digital media 68–9
IIPC (International Internet Preservation Consortium) 73–4, 78, 131
images
  3D 18
  bitmapped 13–16
  digital, selection 34
  vector 16–18
Indiana University, Digital Preservation Unit (workflows) 160
ingest 53, 84–5
input and output pipeline (workflow design) 155–6 (*see also* automation)
intellectual property management *see* IPM
International Internet Preservation Consortium *see* IIPC
International Standard Bibliographic Description *see* ISBD
Internet Archive 74, 76, 77, 78, 170
IPM (intellectual property management) 135–6
Irish Architectural Archive, acquisitions policy 42–3
ISAD(G) General International Standard Archival Description 95
ISBD (International Standard Bibliographic Description) 94
Islandora (online access platform) 146

KryoFlux (disk imaging software) 61, 161, 166, 167

legal and copyright restrictions (access) 133–5
linked data, selection 34, 94
Linux operating system 56, 161, 171, 172
long-lived media (digital preservation and storage) 117–18

Machine Readable Cataloguing *see* MARC
MAD, UK (Manual of Archival Description) 98–9
magnetic media (digital storage media) 23–4, 165–6
management of born-digital materials *see* workflows
Manual of Archival Description *see* MAD, UK
MARC (Machine Readable Cataloguing) 91–3, 94, 102, 103, 104
Massachusetts Institute of Technology (MIT) Institute Archives Records (Collections Policy) 40–1
metadata 42, 65
  certification 121, 122
  disk images 62, 63
  Dublin Core 100
  PREMIS 100–1, 103, 105
  selection 34
  websites and webcrawlers 73, 74
Microsoft Word 33, 116, 142, 143, 149
Minecraft 32, 36 (*see also* computer and video games; virtual spaces)
mission statements 37–8
  Forestry Research Institute of Ghana Library 38
  NASA Space Science Data Coordinated Archive (NSSDCA) 39–40
  National Archives of Japan 38
  specific to digital 38–40
  World Digital Library (WDL) 39
  (*see also* collection policies)
mobile devices, selection 34–5
  (*see also* apps; smartphones)

NASA Space Science Data Coordinated Archive (NSSDCA) mission statement 39–40
National Archives of Japan, mission statement 38
National Digital Stewardship Alliance (NDSA) 115
natural language processing *see* NLP
network-born materials
  access, original order 140
  acquisition of 71, 112
  e-mail 78–81
  existing web archives 78
  on-demand capture 76–8
  social media 81–3
  web crawlers 74–6
  websites 72–4, 75, 76
New Technology File System (NTFS) 55
NLP (natural language processing) 170
normalisation 133

OAIS (Open Archival Information System) 121–3
Omeka (online access platform) 146
on-demand capture
  Archive-It 47–8, 77, 160
  network-born materials 76–8
  Wayback Machine 48, 49, 76–7
  Webrecorder.io 77–8, 82
online access platforms
  BitCurator Access 146
  Drupal 146
  DSpace 146
  Islandora 146
  Omeka 146
  Preservica Universal Access 103, 146–7
  Samvera 147
on-site access 147–8
Open Archival Information System *see* OAIS
optical media (digital storage media) 24–5
original order (access) 54, 139–42, 143

password-protected files 136 (*see also* encryption)
PDF (Portable Document Format) files 33, 72, 73, 145
personally identifying information (PII) 89, 133, 134
physical media information (access) 89
policies excluding digital content 43–4
policies including digital content 41–2
Portable Document Format files *see* PDF
PREMIS (element set) 100–1, 105 (*see also* checksums and checksum algorithms; fixity data)
preservation *see* digital preservation
Preservica Universal Access (online access platform) 103,, 146–7
Princeton University, Library, Department of Rare Books and Special Collections (workflow) 160
programming languages and coding 170, 171, 172, 173
PRONOM (UK National Archives' technical registry) 88, 100, 114, 131, 189

RAD (Rules for Archival Description) 95–7
RDA (Resource Description and Access) 93–4, 102
regex strings 133–4
relational databases *see* databases
remote and restricted online access 147
rendering software 88
repositories
  code 9, 28–9
  digital 103, 115–16
Resource Description and Access *see* RDA
respect des fonds 53–4, 61
risk assessment programmes *see* certification

Rules for Archival Description *see* RAD

Samvera (online access platform) 147
scripting 171, 172 (*see also* command line operations; write blocking)
Second Life (virtual world) 32, 36
selection
  3D modelling, animation and rendering software 32
  audio recordings 33
  books 33
  computer and video games 35–6
  data visualisation 36
  digital documents 33
  digital images 34
  e-books 33–4
  electronic journals 34
  e-mail 34
  feed lists and playlists 35
  format versus content-driven collecting decisions 36–7
  linked data 34, 94
  metadata 34
  mobile devices 34–5
  relational databases 33
  social media 35
  software 35
  spreadsheets 35
  video files 35
  virtual spaces 36
  websites 36
  (*see also* collecting policies; donor agreements; gift agreements; mission statements)
shell software 171–2
'significant properties' (access) 137–8
SIP (Submission Information Package) 121–2
smartphones 168–9 (*see also* apps; mobile devices)
social media 33, 35
  acquisition 81–3, 112
Society of American Archivists 50
software
  3D modelling, animation and rendering 32
  disk imaging 63, 161, 166, 167
  e-mail management and processing 81
  file extraction 64, 114
  hex editors 64–6
  preservation 35, 167
  rendering 88
  selection 35
  shell 171–2
  Software Preservation Network 35, 167
  workflows 153–4, 156–7
  write blocking software 59
solid-state storage media (digital storage media) 25–6, 165–6
Sourceforge (code repository) 28
spreadsheets 20, 35, 156, 158
SQL (Structured Query Language) 33
Stanford University, collection development guidance for web archiving 46–9
Structured Query Language *see* SQL

Submission Information Package *see* SIP

technological infrastructure and restrictions (access) 135–6
third-party materials in arrange ment and context 143–4

UML (Unified Modelling Language) 154
Unicode standard 12, 17
Unified Modelling Language *see* UML
University of Alabama at Birmingham (UAB) Libraries, collections policy 42
University of Colorado Boulder Special Collections, Archives and Preservation Gift Agreement 44–6
University of Leicester Library, collecting policy 43–4
University of Melbourne 54
University of Victoria Libraries, collections policy 41
Unix operating systems 171–2, 193–5

vector images 16–18
video 19–20, 35
video games *see* computer and video games
Vim editor 27, 28, 195
virtual spaces 36 (*see also* computer and video games)

Wayback Machine (on-demand capture) 48, 49, 76–7
web archives and archiving 46–9, 71–8
Web Content Accessibility Guidelines 138
web crawlers 74
  HTTrack 75
  wget 75–6
Webrecorder.io (on-demand capture) 77–8, 82
websites 22
  acquisition 71–4
  existing web archives 78
  in-browser save 72–3
  on-demand capture 76–8
  selection 36
  Web Archive Container (WARC format) 73–4, 75, 76
  web browsers 72
  (*see also* network-born materials)
wget (web crawler) 75–6
WordPerfect 97, 98, 112, 129, 148, 149
WordPress (online access platform) 146, 147
workflow design
  automation 157–8
  audience 154–5
  Denver Art Museum (DAM) workflow example 161–2
  flexibility 158–9
  Indiana University, Digital Preservation Unit, workflow example 160
  input and output pipeline 155–6
  more product less process (MPLP) approach 159

and policy 159–60
Princeton University, Library, Department of Rare Books and Special Collections (workflow example) 160
software 153–4, 156–7

World Digital Library (WDL), mission statement 39
World of Warcraft 32
write blocking 56–61 (*see also* command line operations; scripting)